Poems by Marjorie Kinnan Rawlings

University Press of Florida

GAINESVILLE TALLAHASSEE TAMPA BOCA RATON
PENSACOLA ORLANDO MIAMI JACKSONVILLE

Poems by

Marjorie Kinnan Rawlings

EDITED BY

Rodger L. Tarr

02 01 00 99 98 97   6 5 4 3 2 1

LIBRARY OF CONGRESS CATALOGING-IN-
PUBLICATION DATA
Rawlings, Marjorie Kinnan, 1896–1953.
[Poems. Selections]
Poems by Marjorie Kinnan Rawlings: songs
of a housewife / edited by Rodger L. Tarr.
p. cm.
Poems originally published between 1926
and 1928 in the Rochester times union
under the by-line Songs of a housewife.
Includes bibliographical references and
index.
ISBN 0-8130-1491-3 (alk. paper)
1. Married women—Poetry. 2. House-
wives—Poetry. 3. Motherhood—Poetry.
4. Nature—Poetry. I. Tarr, Rodger L.
II. Title.
PS3535.A845A6 1997
811'.52—dc21   96-50245

Frontispiece: Marjorie Kinnan
Rawlings in the late 1920s.

Page viii and back cover: Clippings
from the Rochester Times-Union,
courtesy of the University of
Florida Libraries, Department of
Special Collections, Marjorie
Kinnan Rawlings Collection.

The University Press of Florida is
the scholarly publishing agency for
the State University System of
Florida, comprised of Florida
A & M University, Florida Atlantic
University, Florida International
University, Florida State Uni-
versity, University of Central
Florida, University of Florida,
University of North Florida,
University of South Florida, and
University of West Florida.

University Press of Florida
15 Northwest 15th Street
Gainesville, FL 32611

To
Gloria and Phil
and
Barb and Bob
friends extraordinaire

The . . . housewife who sets before her family on Thanksgiving Day a perfectly roasted goose, is an artist.

WILLA CATHER, 1927

SONGS of a HOUSEWIFE

ALWAYS HUNGRY.
By Marjorie K. Rawlings.

My children always say they're
  "starved."
You'd think they'd never had
  enough!
You'd think, when we go in to town,
They'd never seen a whipped cream
  puff!

They flatten noses, hands and cheeks
  Against the bakers' windowpanes.
When buttered popcorn fills the air,
  They're accurate as weather-vanes!

Mid-morning, middle-afternoon,
  It's "Can't we have a bite to eat?"
To satisfy those appetites
  Would be a superhuman feat!

I sometimes fear that on my grave
  My tombstone will be harshly
  carved:
"She must have failed her little ones.
  They were always hungry, always
  starved!"
       (Copyright, 1926.)

SONGS OF A HOUSEWIFE
by Marjorie K. Rawlings

DOWN THE PIKE.

When I was young, the nicest folks
Lived down a long road lined with
  oaks.
But grown-ups, shrugging, used to say,
"Oh, they live down the pike a way."

The houses down the pike were dusty,
The curtains drab and torn and musty,
But those who lived there seemed to
  me
Delightful, careless, gay and free.

I liked each low, ramshackle cabin,
Bordered 'round with ragged-robin,
Where children played without a rule,
And didn't have to go to school!

I've treasured for long years the
  thought,
Not of living where I ought,
But living, carefree, where I'd like—
Dusty, happy, down the pike!
      (Copyright, 1927.)

SONGS of a HOUSEWIFE

DUSTING.
By Marjorie K. Rawlings.
(Requested by Mrs. Maud M. A.)

The dust upon my table,
  The dust upon my chairs,
Is blown in from the highway,
  Where all the great world fares.

I need to dust each morning,
  To keep my small house neat,
And I am often wearied
  By all those passing feet.

But where a house is dustless,
  That house is lone and chill,
And no one ever passes,
  And the road is always still.

So as I do my dusting,
  I think, Why should I sigh?
A dusty house is friendly,
  For folks are going by!
      (Copyright, 1926.)

SONGS OF A HOUSEWIFE
by Marjorie K. Rawlings

DRESSING FOR SCHOOL.
(Suggested by Mrs. Muriel E. E.)

Now bless me, only yesterday
I know I put clean shirts away,
But Tommy, dressing on the run,
Declares there's not a single one.

The twins are dawdling with their
  socks,
Oblivious of the speeding clock—
And then there'll be a tumbling rush
To grab the toothpaste, comb and
  brush!

The cocoa and the toast grow cold,
The warning bell just now has
  tolled—
And there's a maudlin scrambling
  'round,
With school books nowhere to be
  found!

No words of reprimand avail,
All modes of discipline fail;
It's natural to make a store
Of what one does not want to do!
      (Copyright, 1927.)

SONGS of a HOUSEWIFE
by Marjorie K. Rawlings

DEVILTRIES

There is a devil! Who else told the twins
To wheel my carpet-sweeper, small Sue on it,
Down our most snobbish street? And for a
  steed,
The hound, unwilling, in a baby bonnet!

And who else put it in their guileless heads
That trees in winter suffer when they're
  bare?
They twined our peach tree with a bolt of
  silk,
And draped the bath towels on our hardy
  pear!

How else did it occur to them to lay
A four-foot snow-man on the register
To warm his hands? To rotate the cat's tail,
To wind her motor up and make her purr?

If these aren't deviltries, to wreck my soul,
My patience and my peace—then black is
  white,
All children angels, and no mother lies
Awake, twixt tears and laughter, half the
  night.
      Copyright, 1927. SFS.

Songs of a Housewife
BY MARJORIE K. RAWLINGS

THE AMATEUR GARDEN.

Last year, remember, we agreed
We'd plant this spring just radish
  seed,
Since nothing else of what we sow
Seems in the least inclined to grow.

Well, try the beans, if you insist.
What's that you're hiding in your
  fist?
Asparagus? That takes two years
Before an edible stalk appears!

Oh, go ahead and plant the peas—
At least the blossoms feed the bees!
Some watermelons? I don't care.
Just stick the beet— anywhere

Merciful Heavens, now we've got
Two dozen varieties in this plot!
The amateur gardener's trusting list
Betrays him the world's prize opti-
  mist!
      (Copyright, 1927.)

CONTENTS

The poems in this book have never been reprinted. In fact, except for very brief references to them found in various texts about Rawlings, they are virtually unknown. They were published from May 24, 1926, through February 29, 1928, in the *Rochester Times-Union* as a regular feature entitled *Songs of a Housewife*. The selection here represents approximately half of the 495 poems published. The divisions, such as "Cooks and Cooking," and the arrangement within the divisions are the editor's. The text is from the newspaper, which is the only authorized text. There is a typescript at the University of Florida, which apparently was made after Rawlings's death in 1953, and which is incomplete and unreliable. The text from the *Times-Union* has not been altered, except where there is an obvious typographical error ("hte" for "the") or an obvious misspelling ("truse" for "truce"). Such errors are corrected silently. All poems are signed either "Marjorie K. Rawlings" or "Marjorie Kinnan Rawlings."

I am especially grateful to Norton S. Baskin, executor of the Rawlings estate, for his encouragement and assistance. For their excellent suggestions regarding the introduction, I am indebted to Peggy Whitman Prenshaw, Kevin M. McCarthy, and Carol A. Tarr. For her inputting of the manuscript, I acknowledge the painstaking work of Irene Taylor; for his careful work on the emendations to the text, I acknowledge Paul Wadden; and, for her splendid copy-editing, I acknowledge Susan Swartwout. The librarians in special collections at Princeton University and at the University of Georgia deserve a special thanks. Carmen Russell Hurff, former curator of the Rawlings Collection at the University of Florida, was of invaluable help. My special debts to Walda Metcalf and to Deidre Bryan will always be remembered. Finally, I gratefully acknowledge those at Illinois State University who administer grants and support research, most notable among them the chair of the English Department, Ronald Fortune, and the dean of the College of Arts and Sciences, Paul Schollaert.

INTRODUCTION

Marjorie Kinnan Rawlings's poems, published under the title *Songs of a Housewife*, belong to that special genre called newspaper poetry. They were addressed, in spirit at least, to the growing working-class readership of the late 1920s. Rawlings's purpose was to entertain, and through entertainment to instruct. The poems, which appeared in the *Rochester Times-Union*, attest not only to her capacity to endure, but also to her capacity to create. The poems were usually, although not always, published six days per week. For almost two years, Rawlings met her deadline. When she stopped writing the column and moved to Florida in 1928, she had written 495 poems on the subject of being a housewife, an achievement unto itself. *Songs of a Housewife*, by all accounts, was immensely popular. At its zenith, it was syndicated in more than fifty newspapers, and thus reached literally thousands of readers each day. The poems were, if one measures the response of Rawlings's readers, a cultural phenomenon. The success of the column stemmed from her ability to identify and then to relate to her audience. *Songs of a Housewife* follows the movement at the turn of the century to take newspapers beyond news, to provide a cultural discourse formed upon entertainment. Newspapers, as Frank Luther Mott points out (583–84), needed to increase circulation. In response, large city newspapers went so far as to employ their own poets, some well known, to write about the contemporary scene. To be sure, some of the poetry is doggerel, hammered out to meet editorial deadlines and local bias.

Yet some of it, depending on the talents of the writer, rises above doggerel. Many of the newspaper poets through local appeal and through syndication became famous, which in turn brought recognition to their respective newspapers. Bert Leston Taylor of the *Chicago Tribune*, Frank P. Adams of the *Chicago Journal*, William D. Nesbit of the *Baltimore American*, and Edgar Guest of the *Detroit Free Press* were among those who brought an air of respectability to newspaper poetry. *Songs of a Housewife* is in the tradition of this respected light verse.

Songs of a Housewife grows out of Rawlings's early commitment to poetry. She began writing poetry as a teenager. The subjects of her juvenilia range from observations on nature to accounts of the supernatural. As a child she was taught by her parents to think independently, to create, not to follow. The result was that early in life she became accomplished at storytelling, a talent that often exhibited itself in recitations of oral tales and poems to delight her peers. At the age of eleven she published her first story in the *Washington Post*, and this was followed by numerous stories and poems, some of which were awarded prizes, usually $2.00, by the newspaper's children's editor.[1] Rawlings attended Western High School, now the Duke Ellington School of the Performing Arts, in Washington, D. C., where she devoted herself to literature and writing. She published in the school literary magazine and the annual yearbook, and she even wrote the school song. In 1911, she published a prize-winning story in *McCall's Magazine*, an accomplishment that seemed to confirm her destiny in letters. After entering the University of Wisconsin in 1914, she continued to exhibit her talents as a writer. Poems flowed from her pen into the pages of university literary publications, most notably the *Wisconsin Literary Magazine*, which she edited her senior year.[2]

Poetry was, in Rawlings's words, "food for the soul." Her commitment to poetry is perhaps most dramatically evidenced in a lead article for the *Wisconsin Literary Magazine*, which she wrote in 1918. With her usual flair for the dramatic, she appealed to her fellow Badgers to give poetry a chance:

But whatever else may be good, one food is guaranteed to bring results. And that? Is poetry. Now, don't stop reading in disgust. Don't you know that poetry may be appetizing as well as nourishing? That, like dentistry, it may be painless, according to the man doing the work? If one dentist hurts unnecessarily, don't you try another? Of course. Why not do the same thing with your poets? Don't condemn them all because the first one makes you sick at your stomach. Poetry can, and should, appeal to "the public." All you need do is start easily, and stick to it. (169)

Rawlings goes on to recommend that neophyte readers should begin with "contemporary poets. Poetry from a modern . . . point of view is bound to be closer to one's own line of thought, than poetry, no matter how magnificent and immortal, of a generation or many generations ago" (169). "Poetry dealing with things of our immediate knowledge," she continues, "voiced in images comprehensible to the modern mind, ought logically be a substantial preparation for poetry in general" (169–70). "Try reading [Vachel] Lindsay," she concludes. "Try other moderns. . . . Expand your poetry-reading as widely and as fast as you can. See if your soul doesn't grow. Just see!" (170). Such an imperative one might expect from a senior whose faculty mentor was William Ellery Leonard, the noted scholar and poet. Rawlings was graduated with honors from the University of Wisconsin in 1918, and a year later was listed in the *Future Poets* series as one of America's promising young poets.

After graduation Rawlings moved to New York City with the same ambition as thousands who came before her, to make her living as a creative writer. Her hopes were soon dashed. No one wanted her creative work, and to survive she had to turn to feature writing for the YWCA. New York, once a mecca of hope, became a forbidding place. In 1919, she married Charles Rawlings, her college sweetheart, and they moved to Louisville, Kentucky. There she gained valuable experience writing features for the *Louisville Courier-Journal* under the byline "Live Women in Live Louisville." These features were far removed from her ambition to be a creative writer.

Each piece, however, does display her creative impulses and her growing commitment to promoting the cause of women. Her poetic career was held in abeyance while she worked for the newspaper. Her letters of the period indicate that when she found time, she did work on her creative writing, but with little or no commercial success. Meanwhile, Charles Rawlings's career floundered, and finally they moved to Rochester, New York, the home of his parents, a move that changed forever Rawlings's literary fortunes.

Rawlings again sought work with a newspaper, this time the *Rochester Times-Union*. She continued to write features, often about the status of women in the marketplace. For a brief period, she also wrote a satirical column for the society magazine *Five O'Clock*.[3] She quickly developed a sense of what was needed—informative advice on divers issues, punctuated with an effort to raise the cultural level of her audience. She began increasingly to employ irony and sarcasm. Her already polished wit sharpened. Early in 1926, she approached the editor of the *Times-Union* with what must have been a startling proposition. She offered to write a poem a day, five days a week, on the subject of the trials and tribulations of being a housewife. The male editor was skeptical at first. Poetry about domestic issues in a newspaper whose subscribership was predominantly working-class did not seem a good idea. Rawlings persisted, and the editor, to her good fortune and to the newspaper's, relented. Publication began on May 24, 1926, and lasted until February 29, 1928, nearly two years and five hundred poems later. The popularity of these poems could not reasonably have been anticipated. In fact, after the publication of the second poem on May 25, the still skeptical editor inserted the following note:

> *This series is an entirely new thought in the feature line, that of making romance of housework. The managing editor of The Times-Union will appreciate a card or letter from you indicating whether you like it.* (26)

For Rawlings to make "romance of housework" was a tall order, indeed. And, as the tenor of this note implies, male editors were still uncertain about the potential problems associated with gender, whether at home or in the marketplace. Hence, the editor's note is more an appeal, founded upon doubt, than an announcement, formed upon conviction.

It was not long, however, before the authorities at the *Times-Union* realized that the column was immensely popular. The letters, judging from the ones that Rawlings chose to reproduce as headers to her poems, must have been overwhelmingly positive. The newspaper felt compelled to introduce formally its new socially responsive poet, and on June 8 a four-column feature was run on Rawlings, replete with pictures, under the header "Where 'Songs Of a Housewife' Were Born," with the suggestive byline "Rochester Girl Discovered That Something as Old as Pots and Pans Could Be Put Into Verse for Benefit of Other Housewives—Reaps Reward of Originality." Insofar as the *Times-Union* was concerned, Rawlings's audience was "Other Housewives." That she is identified as a "Rochester Girl," even though she was thirty years old, speaks for itself. In the article, the editor first expresses how difficult it is for feature editors to find new material, something different, something unusual. He then describes how the "bright and intelligent" Rawlings showed him samples of her work, and, although he was reluctant initially, the idea quickly grew upon him. "Here for the first time," declared the editor, "somebody has discovered that 'housework' can be glorified." Readers were asked for opinions: "These came slowly at first, gradually increasing, and at last became a flood: the women like 'Songs of a Housewife' and they shall have them, for a while anyway. Perhaps a great many other papers will have them, later" (29). "Later" came quickly; within a short time, *Songs of a Housewife* was syndicated throughout the United States, and instead of the letters coming solely from Rochester readers, they came from admirers throughout the nation.

Whether *Songs of a Housewife* was born out of commitment, necessity, or both is not clear. Rawlings is unusually silent on the subject, except for the following quote from the June 8 *Times-Union* interview.[4] Here in full is what she told the editor:

I was brought up to believe in the modern myth that housekeeping is only drudgery, and the housewife is a downtrodden martyr. I thought that any seemingly contented housewives were only "making the best of it." When I first began housekeeping in my own home, I felt that I had entered the ranks of the mistreated.

After a time I began to realize, to my amazement, that I didn't feel at all downtrodden, and that I was thoroughly enjoying myself. I began to look at other domestic "martyrs" from a new angle, and I have learned many things.

I have found that there is a romance in housework: and charm in it; and whimsy and humor without end. I have found that the housewife works hard, of course—but likes it. Most people who amount to anything do work hard, at whatever their job happens to be. The housewife's job is home-making, and she is, in fact, "making the best of it"; making the best of it by bringing patience and loving care to her work; sympathy and understanding to her family; making the best of it by seeing all the fun in the day's incidents and human relationships.

The housewife realizes that home-making is an investment in happiness. It pays enormous dividends. There are huge compensations for the actual labor involved. It will always be so: as long as human beings live together and eat and sleep and wear clothes. Even if community kitchens develop, and community nurseries, women will get a fundamental satisfaction out of making men comfortable and well-fed, and children well "brought up."

With these things in mind, the little incidents of daily housekeeping life began to be worth thinking about. And being a writer, I began to put them into verse. I called them "Songs of a Housewife." As I struggled one day with leathery pie-crust, the thought amused me that, while I was proud of my pie-making ancestors, I wouldn't be expected to turn out perfect pastry if I had descended from a line, say, of savages! There is a verse in that.

There are verses in almost everything that fills a housewife's day.

There may even be one, although I haven't dared write it yet in the iceman, who I am sure waits up the road until I have put a cake in

the oven, and then comes bursting in with a generous cake of ice, good
fellow, on my shaky kitchen floor!
   There are unhappy housewives, of course. But there are unhappy
stenographers and editresses and concert singers. The housewife whose
songs I sing as I go about my work, is the one who likes her job. (29)

Rawlings is forthright. She thinks that housework, in spite of its travails, is constructive work. Of even more importance, she viewed the housewife's role as essential, one founded upon a rich and enduring tradition. By embracing the work of a housewife, Rawlings is, of course, not suggesting that those who choose to work outside the home are less worthy. Quite the contrary. She was fully committed to a woman's right to share equally in the workplace, and boldly advocated "community nurseries," day care centers, to protect that right. Yet she took the firm position that women who choose to stay at home are also professionals. To be sure, the rewards are different, but it is her strong conviction, one she never abandoned, that housewives do not bring shame upon womanhood.

   In a dramatic way, then, Rawlings was addressing a new class of American woman, what Nancy Cott has called the "modern American woman" (76). Largely because of the feminist tradition that immediately preceded them, middle-class women in the 1920s were now asserting their rights, demanding equality not only in the workplace but in the home as well. This cultural revolution was given impetus by the technical revolution. The housewife was provided with all manner of new technologies designed to make life at home easier. Washers, refrigerators, even the electric light switch, which General Electric boldly claimed was linked to suffrage, were emblems of the "new housekeeping." Advertisers quickly exploited the emerging modern woman, and the cinema idealistically portrayed the new housewife. As Cott observes, "No longer diffident, delicate, and submissive, the ideal modern woman was portrayed as vigorous and gregarious." Commercialism, Cott concludes, "absorbed the challenges of feminism and re-represented them in the form of the modern American woman" (89–90).

New-found freedoms were not without a toll, however. Instead of lessening the burden of the housewife, these freedoms created an awareness that actually made more difficult and more complicated the housewife's role. Social scientists and governmental agencies issued myriad studies to make the housewife more aware of her responsibilities, and in doing so made it more difficult for her to fulfill them. Studies indicate that the typical housewife worked between thiry-five and fifty hours per week. Ironically, technology increased rather than lessened the psychological as well as the physical burden of the housewife. And, of course, more and more women were choosing to work outside the home, which further complicated the issues surrounding housewives and the divers roles played by them. Thus, beneath the rose-colored picture of the ideal woman in the 1920s lay tensions as yet unresolved and conflicts newly created. In *Songs of a Housewife*, Rawlings addresses these tensions and conflicts with practical advice and homespun philosophy.

Since *Songs of a Housewife* comprises nearly five hundred poems, it is difficult to categorize them. They are eclectic, embrace a diverse vision, and are articulated through an often complex narrator who represents multiple experiences. However, on one point Rawlings's opinion never varies: Housewives, as she declares in "Getting Meals" (December 13, 1926), deserve "sainthood." She believes there is reward for hard work, although one of the humorous crosscurrents is her penchant for avoiding necessary work for creative accomplishment. She would rather bake a pie than dust a table, or arrange a bouquet than scrub the floor, or cook a full dinner than wash the dishes. One is creative and the other is not. Rawlings uses her experiences as the prism for her readers' experiences. She knows, for example, that it is human nature to be dilatory, to put off until tomorrow chores that should have been done today. In *Songs of a Housewife* she exploits her idiosyncrasies, many of which, of course, are ours. Rawlings procrastinates; we all procrastinate. Rawlings is impatient; we all are impatient. Rawlings loves okra; we all love . . . well, maybe. This is the curious thing about *Songs of a Housewife*: the poems are deeply personal, yet expressly universal. We do not have to relish okra to like the poems, but we must like food, or at least certain foods, for Rawlings consistently views housework from a number of culinary perspectives. We do not have to like noisy neighbors, but we have to like neighborly fellowship, again usually expressed through culinary metaphor. Not all chores are glorified, however. Rawlings despises ironing, ranking it somewhere between mending socks and cleaning the toilet. Yet she is consistent in conviction. She tries to live by the golden rule and succeeds, most of the time. And she never wavers in her belief in the dignity of work.

Rawlings does have favorite topics, however. Food, both the cooking of it and the eating of it, is primary. Indeed, culinary principles are at the heart of *Songs of a Housewife*. Such investment will come as no surprise to those who have read her fiction. In *Cross Creek* (1942), she recounts how difficult it was for her to learn the art of cooking, and how much it meant in her marriage to Charles Rawlings, from whom she was divorced in 1933, who had once thrown hollandaise sauce in her face because it was not prepared properly. Rawlings's bitterly satiric short story "The Pelican's Shadow" (1940) reveals the psychological damage that resulted from this and similar episodes. Her *Cross Creek Cookery* (1942) might be seen as a psychological working out of the traumas she once suffered. Certainly, it displays a wit born out of the necessity to cook with humor and with grace. In many respects, *Songs of a Housewife* is her first cookbook, replete with wise and pithy nostrums on human nature. It is not surprising that her first poem is on the importance of food. "The Smell of Country Sausage" (May 24, 1926) deliciously reminds us that the aroma of country sausage "Beats any breakfast bell / For routing out the sleepy-heads— / It means hot cakes as well." The poem is matter-of-fact, to be sure; however, hidden not too far below the surface is the message that we all are quite willing to avoid the duties of life until we are stimulated into action, here by the smell of sausage and the thought of "buckwheat cakes and syrup / As thick as Jersey cream." Culinary metaphors expressing philosophic meanings are central to all of Rawlings's canon, but to the *Songs of the Housewife* they are critical.[5]

As Rawlings takes us through every conceivable cooking situation, it is clear from the number of poems devoted to the subject that she prefers pastry cooking the most and preparing lunch the least, no doubt because lunch normally allows less room for experimentation. Still, any meal is a good meal if it is properly prepared with love and consideration. So devoted is Rawlings to the art of cooking that she on occasion guards the secrets of certain recipes. For example, in "Secrets," she relates that she is especially "noted" for her pumpkin pie: "The flavor of my pumpkin pie / Is touted far and wide. / Why then reveal, betray my art, / The secrets of my pride?" (November 18, 1926). Again, we are presented with an underlying social dilemma. Rawlings is willing to convict herself for being a "selfish thing" for not sharing the recipe, but she still declines the entreaties of the curious, for she instinctively knows that her "pride" will become the recipient's if she divulges her secret. Yet such guarding of one's culinary identity is the exception rather than the rule. Rawlings repeatedly articulates the need for sharing, which she sees as a form of social affection. In "Swapping Recipes" (October 30, 1926), she assures the reader that a "woman's dearest pleasure / Is swapping recipes!" Rawlings is reflecting here the practice of women coming together, sharing recipes, and in doing so establishing a bond, a bond she explores from a different perspective in "Samaritans Needed" (March 2, 1927).

Rawlings extends her common-sense culinary morality to all manner of food stuffs. Cooking is an art and she is the artist. In "A Kitchen Artist" (April 14, 1927), she defends her messy kitchen by asking, "Do artists at their canvases / Pause to clean the room? / Do sculptors at their modeling / Keep one hand on the broom?" Her reasoning is logical enough: "I am a kitchen artist— / I cannot cramp my style!" In "Born Cooks" (January 19, 1928), she sees the cook as innately artistic: "The love of cooking fills her heart / As poets are filled with love of song. / She weeps when custard-pies go wrong— / An artist for the sake of art!" Rawlings is especially devoted to creative cooking: the bringing together of "odds-and-ends" from a "pantry bare and clean" is a mark of one's abilities as a chef, as discussed in "A Meal of Almost Nothing" (February 8, 1928). As she reminds us in "On the Job" (February 13, 1928), when she cooks,

"My reputation is at stake." Food can bring people together, heal wounds, and erase old enmities; Rawlings especially favors pies, which, as in the case of "A Very Useful Pie" (August 11, 1927), "Made of my enemy, a friend!" Rawlings's moral points regarding the use of food are clear. She never is trivial. Food is the impetus for thought: "How thoughts mingle, over the food!" she muses in "At Breakfast" (December 5, 1927). Whether Rawlings is sharing, however reluctantly, a recipe for gingerbread, a hint for the use of spice, or the secret of an excellent roast, she does so in an unassuming manner, as a friend as well as an advisor. Her moral recipes are invariably offered through the voice of friendship.

Nature is another of Rawlings's favorite topics. Nature is a representation of God's favor, although God as a concept seldom enters directly into her poems. Instead, she relies upon faith, which she sees as a transcendental force that runs through nature. There is a large element of Thoreau in Rawlings, an element she later expanded upon in *The Yearling* and *Cross Creek*. She is a proponent of natural splendor. Nature is divine, or at least a reflection of divinity. A committed environmentalist, Rawlings not only seeks beauty, she seeks to preserve beauty. Her message is constant: nature is an emblem of eternity.[6] Day and night, sunshine and darkness, April and December have a divinity. Gardens are nature's glory; nut trees, nature's nectar. Rawlings's descriptions of nature are sensual. Fully half her poems involve nature in some manner; flowers are her special love. Rose blossoms, lilacs, and sweet peas are all celebrated for their special fragrances.

All seasons, not just fall, are seasons of fruitfulness. If she were forced to choose, however, Rawlings's favorite time of year is spring, "when April's at the full," as described in "A Rendezvous" (October 11, 1926). In "Earth's Children" (November 29, 1927), "leaves and fruits and flowers" plant their seeds, and in the spring "Earth is repaid for all her love and toil." In "Spring Tonics" (March 26, 1927), "Beauty has powers medicinal / To make the spirit whole"; in "Sitting in the Sun" (April 1, 1927), spring's warm sun brings on "Thoughts all hazy— / Dinner late— / Isn't it lazy— / And isn't it great!"; and in "Spring Is a Housewife" (May 9, 1927), when spring

"brings out song and sun, / Decks out the world with posies gay—
/ Her housewife's job is done!" In the end, it is nature that restores
us, particularly in hours of stress and trial. In "A Kitchen Facing
West" (May 17, 1927), Rawlings writes of the restorative power of
nature. As her "trials increase" and as her "mind grows tired and
dull," she observes: "Then through my westward window-pane /
The sun streams in across my floor, / My table, in a golden rain— /
And I can smile and sing once more!" The natural, as well as the
spiritual, message contained in these lines is typical of Rawlings's
reverence for nature. As always, however, she exercises her humor,
complaining in an ironic tone in "The Lucky Housewife" (January
7, 1928): "Dame Nature stops work in the Fall / And doesn't tidy
things at all. / . . . / Alas, when I leave my debris / Strewn up and
down for all to see, / No miracles hover, / My sins to cover / And
hide my carelessness for me!"

Rawlings also deals extensively with human affection, especially
motherhood and family relationships. In fact, one of the accom-
plishments of *Songs of a Housewife* is the manner in which Rawlings
creates a family unit over which she is the matriarch. For her to
identify with motherhood so deeply, without having experienced it,
is a notable achievement, although readers familiar with her classic
short story "A Mother in Mannville" (1936) will not be surprised.
Rawlings's family in *Songs of a Housewife* is made up of a daughter,
Sue; a son, Tom; and the twins, who are not given names. Aunts,
uncles, cousins, and even a grandmother appear, and each is given a
name and an identity. Curiously, no father appears, although there
is no criticism, stated or implied, of fatherhood. Rawlings's devo-
tion to children is especially apparent in the poems. In one of her
earliest poems, "Loving" (June 10, 1926), she worries about what
would happen if her love was not returned by her children, and
then asks: "Without their love, could I endure to live?" Her advice
to mothers who experience similar feelings is to redouble their giv-
ing, for such love is "A woman's serving, her beatitude." Such devo-
tion is prepared for in "Making the Beds," the poem written the day
before: "They will sleep here tonight, so let me give / What time
and life conspire to take away: / Slumber made smooth and sweet

by hands that live / Only to love and serve them every day." In one of her last poems, "A Full House" (February 4, 1928), she is blunt. To choose not to have children is a "stupid choice," for everyone knows "A full house beats a pair!" How much of Rawlings's own persona is invested in this language we can never know. Still, her refrain remains unchanged: "A full house beats a pair!"

It could be argued that Rawlings through her celebration of motherhood is unwittingly condemning women to familial servitude. True, Rawlings's projections of motherhood are sometimes idealistic and to an extent self-serving. She could hardly be expected to criticize motherhood in a column largely addressed to housewives, many of whom were mothers or prospective mothers. In the main, however, she is realistic when it comes to rearing children and dealing with domestic chores. In "Twins" (June 16, 1926), she remarks with a twinge of irony: "I didn't think of holes in socks / When I prayed for twins!" But such regret is not long-lived. In the concluding stanza, she returns to her cheerful position: "They're twice the standard mixture / Of monkey, imp and dove. / There's twice as much small boy to scold— / But twice as much to love!" Yet, because Rawlings's poetic children are more often than not hellions, she advocates in "Bedlam" (June 9, 1927) that there be instituted a "Be-Kind-To-Housewives-Week" to recognize patience as a virtue among mothers. In her household, the twins have a "cross old cat" and Tom has "a parrot / With an evil beak," and the result is predictable: "The boys and the animals / Shriek and race, / 'Til there's riotous bedlam / All over the place." Rawlings's exasperation reaches fever pitch in "Hoodlums" (July 5, 1927), when she despairs that "Tom and the twins are a constant disgrace, / Tattered of breeches and dirty of face." Her descriptions of the nightmares mothers encounter as they face the daily ritual of mothering are compelling. Motherhood is difficult, perhaps the most difficult of professions, Rawlings concludes. In "Almost" (August 10, 1927), she describes the children's "squabbles ringing in my ear" and her thought to "Pack up my bag and take to flight." But when the children ask, "'And would you really run away?' / I smile and hug them. 'Ah—almost!'" Christmas is, of course, the season children enjoy most, and "A Glimpse of Santa" (December 14, 1927) is a charming poem about the wonder-filled creeping of children down the stairs, "Shivering in the dawn with hope and fear, / To see if Santa Claus had yet been there." In a later poem, "Uncle Abner" (December 20, 1927), Christmas is described as a poignant time, for this year the family is confronted with the absence of Uncle Abner, once the "finest Kriss," who now lives in Heaven and plays Santa to the cherubim. Here, the inevitability and the pain of death strike home.

Rawlings's poetic family extends beyond Tom, Sue, and the twins to include all manner of folk. There is Uncle Lou and Aunt Em Seaton, whom we meet in "The Family Album" (February 9, 1927) with their "twelve offspring" pictured "side by side." Later these cousins are reduced to seven, four of whom are given names, "Bill and Jim and Tom and Ed," and described in "Company's Coming!" (August 19, 1927). The Seaton clan appears most frequently, but there is also Aunt Nelly and Uncle Bill, who, in "Pleasing Everybody" (March 29, 1927), are described as finicky, especially Uncle Bill, who, during the carving of the roast, makes Rawlings's heart stand still: "Is it too well done for Uncle Bill?" A visit from the elegant Aunt Janette, whom we meet only once in "The Horrors" (June 20, 1927), frightens Rawlings with the thought that that there might not be "Enough clean tea-towels for the dinner dishes!" Uncle Eb and Aunt Emmy, whom we also meet only once, appear in "My Friend's Relations" (January 20, 1928), the title of which tells the whole story. Aunt Annie appears once as well, in "Baby Sue's Bath" (June 18, 1926).

There is also a whole host of friends and neighbors, who are introduced by name, and who in many ways foreshadow the friends and neighbors who appear later in *Cross Creek*. Jim and Miranda Perkins appear the most often. Miranda is renowned for her "Braised southern chicken, golden-brown, / With sweetbreads for a border," only to be heartbroken when she learns that Jim prefers beans from a local restaurant: "The best-fed, petted, pampered men," says Rawlings, "Most feel the need for change!" (February 22, 1927). Minerva Jenkins, the town eccentric, who "Goes unobserved of men" until "She puts an apron on," allows Rawlings to deal with beauty of countenance and beauty of performance, the last always being the yardstick against which people should be measured, as discussed in "Handsome Is as Handsome Does" (June 3, 1927). The legendary Mis' Meekin, whose "knotted hands" are "rough and clean as tree-bark scrubbed by rain," is introduced with requisite envy in "Mis' Meekin's Dumplings" (February 12, 1927). "Crazy Nell" (September 1, 1927) speaks of madness with the ironic twist at the end: "'Can madness be where beauty is?'" In "The Gadabout" (August 18, 1927), Susan Jenks is introduced as the person who can always get Rawlings to procrastinate and then to worry openly: "I think I must be feeble-minded!" The Scotsman Dan M'Groun, in "The Jesters" (September 3, 1927), causes frustration, principally because he is able to imitate expertly the sound of birds calling and thus deceive the townspeople. "Neighbors" (June 17, 1926) sums up the innate goodness Rawlings finds in all people, no matter first appearances: Miss Perkins is a "fearful cat" until she brings the sick baby soothing "goose-fat"; the doctor's wife is "quite a snob" until she brings the ailing Rawlings her "first Russell rose"; and Miss Smith "complains about my boys," but brings "broth when they had mumps."

It is clear that Rawlings's fictive models are based, in part at least, on real people, a technique she employed later with great effect in her fiction. In one case an actual person, Rawlings's beloved Aunt Ida, is celebrated in a poem ("Aunt Ida's Letters," December 4, 1926). The Rawlings circle of family and friends is full, and the number of poems devoted to the circle attests to the concern for human foibles and frailties found throughout *Songs of a Housewife*. Rawlings's kinship with her audience is formed upon subjects such as friendship and loyalty, duty and love, and age and death. In fact, fully two-thirds of her poems are on these subjects or related ones, such as jealousy and envy, patience and order, procrastination and vanity. Of the importance of friendship, she writes in "Sunday Night Tea" (June 5, 1926) about the thrill of serving guests, "Since with their friendship they are serving me." In "Dusting" (August 24, 1926), she makes a positive connection between dustiness and friendship: "A dusty house is friendly," for "where a house is dustless, / That house is lone and chill." The appeal here joins neatly the social need for friends and the social reality of procrastination. Rawlings is forever admitting her foibles and then justifying them within the context of human frailty. In "Old Clothes" (September 16, 1926), when a reader, Mrs. Nelly C., writes in to ask, "Can't you find some consolation in having to wear old clothes when we long for new ones?" Rawlings responds within the context of friendship: "For lovely clothes would not assure / A neighbor's warm and kindly smile. / Old friends forgive old clothes, because / Friendship is never out of style!" Rawlings repeatedly reminds her readers that the core of human association is friendship, and that a true friend is welcomed any time, but "Morning Friends" (September 20, 1926) are the "nearest and the dearest." As she concludes in "The Festal Board" (October 18, 1926), any table is a "festal / When friendly folks sit there!" Friendship transcends hypocrisy, as she insists in "Friends Who Drop In" (February 21, 1927), "Friends who drop in are simply there / Because they want to come!" Indeed, friends can be those who drop in unannounced, "Such friendly interruptions / Are pleasanter than work," she confesses in "Interruptions" (April 21, 1927).

Friendship also extends beyond personal acquaintanceship to those "Friends by Sight" (November 15, 1926), for "They come from nowhere, and they go / Unknown and nameless, day and night. / But life is sweeter for the nods, / The passing, of my friends-by-sight." This vision of friendship extends to age and death. In "Sunset and Friends" (December 14, 1926), Lillian E. E. writes to Rawlings, "I do not entirely agree with Mary C. B. on the subject of growing old. When I am old I do not want to live alone. I love the friends about me. What is your way of expressing this?" Rawlings responds, "I would not be alone when sunset ends, / For love alone can quench the spirit's thirst. / The years bring wisdom—and that wisdom, friends." Love and friendship are inviolate; one cannot exist without the other. In "Your Way and Mine" (January 15, 1927), she addresses concerns raised by separation: "Friendship is of the heart, / The mind and the soul; / Lives may drift far apart, / But love stays whole." In "Hospitality" (July 28, 1927), we learn that "Finer than open hands," is the "open heart." Rawlings expresses succinctly in

"'Dear Friend'" (March 7, 1927) the value of friendship while apart: "And always these two words shall be / A seal for friendship to the end: / A loving bond for you and me, / And sweet upon the ear: 'Dear Friend'." The subject of friendship, among what I would designate her philosophical poems, is often treated in a serious tone in *Songs of a Housewife*.

Usually, however, Rawlings's sense of humor serves as a foil for her seriousness. She understands that most of life is a comedy of errors, and she writes in a light spirit about those everyday occurrences that reveal our fallibility. We are creatures of comfort, Rawlings opines. When we are uncomfortable, we are unhappy; when we are comfortable, we are happy. Caught in the middle of this domestic comedy is the housewife who must daily confront and solve life's problems. What happens to the night's meal if the stove suddenly misfires; what happens to the children's clothes if the washer malfunctions; indeed, what happens to the cake in the oven when the iceman drops a heavy block of ice on the floor? Rawlings's poems are filled with such domestic tragedy. Dogs wet on carpets; cats tear curtains; hogs root spring gardens; children leave toys under foot; and adults ignore the most civil of duties, the wiping of feet before entering upon a newly scrubbed floor. Noise annoys; silence infuriates. Strangers interrupt; guests demand too much. Friends sympathize; maids disappoint. No domestic situation is too slight to escape Rawlings's scrutiny. The housewife is the most put upon of human beings. She is expected to cook, to sew, to clean, and most of all, to love. If a housewife is also a mother, she is confronted with conflicting roles that require unusual patience.

Rawlings expresses amazement at such accomplishment, particularly since such virtues seldom are achieved without personal sacrifice. Yet she refuses to see housewives as martyrs to meaningless causes. Housewives are keepers of the faith, creators of noble deeds, principals of compassion. Each housewife, says Rawlings, in "A Housewife's Luxuries" (August 20, 1927), is an artist with an "artist's soul." In one of the last poems, "A Housewife's Hands" (February 7, 1928), Rawlings locates the housewife in the eternity of the past. What comprises, she asks, a "housewife's skill"? "Not so much practice o'er and o'er, / But that the eternal housewife stands / Behind me—those who went before / With age-old, quick, maternal hands." What is her reward? Rawlings tells us in "The Housewife's Heaven" (February 27, 1928): "A world full of love to remind her of home, / With a 'spat', for the good of her soul, now and then, / And oh, the vast markets of Heaven to comb / For foods to delight cherubs, angels and men!"

Songs of a Housewife gains dignity of purpose and clarity of design in part because Rawlings is able to link her sense of values to her sense of humor, which culminates in her sense of audience. This is not to imply, however, that she is an accomplished poet, at least as defined by the "great tradition" of the academy. Students of poetry will not come to Rawlings to study the art of poetry, but they could learn much from her about the effect of a certain genre of poetry. Scholars might lament certain infelicities in language and meter, and pundits might even question the value of reprinting such poems. Yet the truth is that *Songs of a Housewife* was not intended for scholars or for pundits. The poems are, in fact, deliberately composed against the grain of the intellectual. There is little of what might be called refinement in them. The printing schedule, if nothing else, precluded that. *Songs of a Housewife* was written for the working class, those educated enough to appreciate humor and wise enough to understand common sense. Rawlings's working-class readers complemented perfectly her talents. They especially appreciated her self-effacing humor, and they very quickly identified with her sentiment and wit. The record clearly indicates that her subjects delighted her readers, perhaps because she always cuts to the heart of her subject. Her metaphors are plain but expressive; her language common but appealing. Sophisticated bons mots, such as those popularized by her contemporary Dorothy Parker, are avoided. Rawlings records the present, the relevant, the possible. Her instruction is given from the heart. There is no posing, no attempt to impress. There can be little doubt that *Songs of a Housewife*, taken in its entirety, is of significant value as a history of a specific culture within a specific time frame.

Yet as much as *Songs of a Housewife* is universal, it is also personal.

We must not overlook the singular "Housewife" in the title. Rawlings makes no pretense to speak for all women, or for all housewives. In many respects, hers is a personal saga. And, this is, in part, the appeal of the poems. They record personal experience. Her voices are clearly her voices, formed, to be sure, on a rich and varied tradition, what Virginia Woolf was referring to when she said of the subtext of women's writing, "We think back through our mothers if we are women" (79). Nevertheless, the appeal of *Songs of a Housewife* is that Rawlings, through the perspective of a particular housewife, is able to represent universal experience. The response of readers to her column testifies to the power of her voice. It is inevitable that *Songs of a Housewife* will be judged as poetry, albeit newspaper verse. But in the end its real impact rests outside the poetic. From May of 1926 until March of 1928, Rawlings was a widely read spokesperson for the American housewife. Her ennobling of this often marginalized class ensures the immortality of these poems. As Peggy Whitman Prenshaw reminds us, ". . . what Rawlings most deeply resented and found personally debilitating—and fought against all her life—was the powerlessness of the average woman, the powerlessness even of exceptional women in her society" (16). Although Prenshaw is reflecting on *Cross Creek*, her words apply equally to the tone set in *Songs of a Housewife*. These poems are a reminder of the dignity of labor manifest in the dignity of woman, here the housewife. *Songs of a Housewife* is a unique cultural record, more so because the poems are written by a woman to women, and for that reason alone they will maintain their cultural and historical importance.

NOTES

1. One of Rawlings's poems, written when she was sixteen ("To James Whitcomb Riley," *Washington Post*, October 27, 1912), is a lengthy celebration that won first prize in the Riley Contest. From 1910 to 1914, the *Post* published twenty-nine poems, short stories, and letters by Rawlings, née Kinnan (see my "Marjorie Kinnan Rawlings and the *Washington Post*," 163-68).

2. For a complete detailing of Rawlings's poems, see my *Marjorie Kinnan Rawlings: A Descriptive Bibliography*. In addition to *Songs of a Housewife*, Rawlings published twenty-two poems and wrote many others. The archives at the University of Florida and the University of Georgia contain a number of poems in various stages of draft. Although she never lost interest in poetry, she turned almost exclusively to fiction during her so-called Florida period (1928–53).

3. Rawlings, under the nom de plume Lady Alicia Thwaite, wrote in 1924 four pieces for *Five O'Clock*, edited by the literary entrepreneur Henry W. Clune. They are instructive in documenting her search for an audience and for a voice. The wit and humor of these prose pieces are similar to that found in *Songs of a Housewife* and suggest things to come (see my "Marjorie Kinnan Rawlings and the Rochester [N.Y.] Magazine *Five O'Clock*").

4. Gordon E. Bigelow in *Frontier Eden: The Literary Career of Marjorie Kinnan Rawlings* claims that Rawlings "dryly remarked years later that the money she made by writing 'Songs of a Housewife' may have enabled her to avoid one kind of prostitution but not another" (8). Bigelow does not cite a source for his claim. Elizabeth Silverthorne, in *Marjorie Kinnan Rawlings: Sojourner at Cross Creek*, repeats this story without citation, no doubt taking it from Bigelow. Whatever the facts are, such postmortems on her work are typical of Rawlings and thus should not be taken seriously. Little critical attention has been given to the poems, largely because of their number and their inaccessibility. Bigelow devotes just a paragraph to them, calling them "cheery, sentimental pieces," a "testimony to her ingenuity and perseverance" (*Frontier Eden*, 7). In the interlinear narrative to their edition of Rawlings's letters, Bigelow and Laura V. Monti refer to them as poems about the "cheery, pleasant side of running a household" (35). Silverthorne, in "Marjorie Kinnan Rawlings: The Early Years," provides a brief commentary, referring to them as "light and cheerful and somewhat Edgar Guestish, often with a sentimental or humorous twist." In her *Marjorie Kinnan Rawlings*, she calls them "slight verses" (53), although she does acknowledge that they were syndicated through United Features and appeared in some fifty newspapers. Samuel Bellman in *Marjorie Kinnan Rawlings* gives them less than a paragraph, pronouncing them "homey little verses" (56). Such limited judgments miss entirely the cultural and historical value of *Songs of a Housewife* and ignore completely the importance of the poems in Rawlings's development as a writer.

5. Rawlings uses cooking as a metaphor in her longer works, but particularly in *The Yearling* (1938) and *Cross Creek* (1942). However, it is in her short fiction, most notably "The Pelican's Shadow," that she often uses it as a con-

trolling metaphor. See *Short Stories of Marjorie Kinnan Rawlings,* ed. Rodger L. Tarr. For a suggestive essay on the subject of cooking as metaphor, see Michael P. Dean, "Recipes, Repasts, and Regionalism: Marjorie Kinnan Rawlings's *Cross Creek Cookery* and 'Our Daily Bread'."

6. Aside from the appeals found throughout her fiction, Rawlings wrote two spirited pieces on ecological concerns: "Florida: A Land of Contrasts" (*Transatlantic*) and "Florida: An Affectionate Tribute" (*Congressional Record*).

BIBLIOGRAPHY

Bellman, Samuel I. *Marjorie Kinnan Rawlings.* New York: Twayne, 1974.

Bigelow, Gordon E. *Frontier Eden: The Literary Career of Marjorie Kinnan Rawlings.* Gainesville: University of Florida Press, 1966.

Cott, Nancy F. "The Modern Woman of the 1920s, American Style." In *A History of Women in the West.* Ed. Françoise Thébaud. Cambridge, Mass.: Belknap Press, 1994. 76–91.

Dean, Michael P. "Recipes, Repasts, and Regionalism: Marjorie Kinnan Rawlings's *Cross Creek Cookery* and 'Our Daily Bread'." In *Cooking by the Book: Food in Literature and Culture.* Ed. Mary Anne Schofield. Bowling Green, Ky.: Bowling Green State University Popular Press, 1989. 107–13.

Mott, Frank Luther. *American Journalism.* Rev. ed. New York: Macmillan, 1950.

Prenshaw, Peggy Whitman. "Marjorie Kinnan Rawlings: Woman, Writer, and Resident of Cross Creek." *Rawlings Journal* 1 (1988): 1–17.

Rawlings, Marjorie Kinnan. *Cross Creek.* New York: Scribner's, 1942.

———. *Cross Creek Cookery.* New York: Scribner's, 1942.

———. "Florida: A Land of Contrasts." *Transatlantic* 14 (1944): 12–17.

———. "Florida: An Affectionate Tribute." *Congressional Record* (U.S. House of Representatives), March 2, 1945, 1692–93.

———. "[On Poetry]." *Wisconsin Literary Magazine* 17 (April 1918): 169–70.

———. *Selected Letters of Marjorie Kinnan Rawlings.* Ed. Gordon E. Bigelow and Laura V. Monti. Gainesville: University Presses of Florida, 1983.

———. *Short Stories of Marjorie Kinnan Rawlings.* Ed. Rodger L. Tarr. Gainesville: University Press of Florida, 1994.

———. *The Yearling.* New York: Scribner's, 1938.

Silverthorne, Elizabeth. "Marjorie Kinnan Rawlings: The Early Years." *Rawlings Journal* 1 (1988): 18–28.

———. *Marjorie Kinnan Rawlings: Sojourner at Cross Creek.* Woodstock, N.Y.: Overlook, 1988.

Tarr, Carol A., and Rodger L. Tarr. Introduction to *Cross Creek*, by Marjorie Kinnan Rawlings. Jacksonville, Fla.: South Moon Books, 1992.

Tarr, Rodger L. *Marjorie Kinnan Rawlings: A Descriptive Bibliography*. Pittsburgh: University of Pittsburgh Press, 1996.

———. "Marjorie Kinnan Rawlings and the *Washington Post*." *Analytical and Enumerative Bibliography*, n.s., 4 (1990): 163–68.

———. "Marjorie Kinnan Rawlings and the Rochester (N.Y.) Magazine *Five O'Clock*." *American Periodicals* 1.1 (1991): 83–85.

Woolf, Virginia. *A Room of One's Own*. 1929. New York: Harcourt, 1957.

Cooks and Cooking

Mother's Cooking

My cakes don't taste like Mother's,
    I've never touched her bread—
But Grandma's plainest cooking
    Excelled her best, she said.

And Grandma said her mother
    Could put great chefs to shame.
Great-grandma was a genius,
    She said, with fowl and game.

I treat my food's praise lightly,
    My family's flattering zest—
For somehow, "Mother's cooking"
    Has always tasted best.

JANUARY 21, 1928

Cooking Confession

I've often said: "Real cooking skill
　　Is never learned at college.
The art of food and drink is based
　　On deep, instinctive knowledge."

Hereditary craft, I've claimed,
　　Down family lines continues:
The true-born cook should feel no need
　　Of recipes or menus.

I like to cook elaborately,
　　"From memory," without blunder.
I like to whip up cheese souffles
　　As guests stand lost in wonder!

But things go wrong so often
　　With this "instinctive" cooking,
That I've a nook for my cook-book—
　　And peek when no one's looking!

JULY 16, 1926

A Kitchen Artist

(Suggested by Mrs. Harry M. G.)

When I do fancy baking,
    My tidy ways take flight.
I dirty every dish I own—
    My kitchen is a sight!

In my creative frenzy
    I use up every pan;
I strew things here and yon and make
    The biggest mess I can.

Do artists at their canvases
    Pause to clean the room?
Do sculptors at their modeling
    Keep one hand on the broom?

I claim the same forbearance
    In time of pastry trial.
I am a kitchen artist—
    I cannot cramp my style!

APRIL 14, 1927

Born Cooks

Good cooks are born, not made. Go train
  Most anyone to boil and bake,
  A cook for pure necessity's sake;
Her food is merely decent, plain.

Your true-born cook will pine and yearn
  To get her hand on this and that—
  A sauce, some greens, a butter-pat;
She never, never lets things burn.

She shaped mud-patties as a child
  And called them pudding, cake and bun;
  Too serious to call it fun,
A mud-pie failure drove her wild.

The love of cooking fills her heart
  As poets are filled with love of song.
  She weeps when custard-pies go wrong—
An artist for the sake of art!

JANUARY 19, 1928

Nose News

I could smell my neighbor's gingerbread,
    Cooling on a shelf.
Its fragrance put it in my head
    To bake a pan myself.

The morning breeze blew down the street
    My gingerbread's spiced whiff.
My other neighbor stayed her feet,
    And paused a bit to sniff.

Before the noon-day whistle blew
    I saw her baking there—
And soon the scent of ginger grew,
    Delicious on the air.

That evening all the men-folks said:
    "Nose news must travel fast.
We could smell fresh gingerbread
    In every house we passed!"

FEBRUARY 13, 1927

Good Pie

The woman who can make good pie
    Stands on her own Gibraltar,
And men will always hover by,
    To lead her to the altar.

The woman who can mix a crust
    As light as gosling's feather,
Need never tread the highway's dust
    Nor feel life's Wintry weather.

Her lemon pie, her coconut,
    Her apple, mince and custard,
Salute her every time they're cut—
    Her guard of honor, mustered!

Tho' she be plain and mousey-mild,
    Her hungry friends adore her;
Pie-loving woman, man and child,
    Prostrate, salaam before her!

FEBRUARY 25, 1927

A Very Useful Pie

I never made a better pie
In all my years of cooking. My!
   It was a golden-brown delight
   And tasted just exactly right!

The crust was flaky, light and thin.
I put enough brown sugar in
   To make it rich past any doubt,
   Yet not so rich it might boil out.

I thought when Mrs. Jenkins came
And ate a piece, it was a shame,
   With pie of such rare delicacy,
   To waste it on an enemy!

But her sharp face grew pleased and kind.
"Some more," she beamed, "if you don't mind."
   That pie's perfection, in the end,
   Made of my enemy, a friend!

AUGUST 11, 1927

Poor Proportions

It takes me half the afternoon,
  And I am no beginner,
To cook the meal that's gone so soon,
  And called a "simple" dinner.

One hour to make the plainest cake,
  For mince pie, two are plenty.
Hundreds of minutes used to make
  A feast folks eat in twenty!

A dinner's disproportionableness
  Daily strikes me stronger,
Of time, the cook should use much less—
  Or the diners should take longer!

JANUARY 31, 1928

Lickin' Good

I've had many kinds of praises
   For jelly, pie and cake.
My friends are most appreciative
   Of everything I make.

"Your marmalade's so delicate!"
   "Your cake grain is so fine!"
One shameless flatterer even said
   My biscuits were divine!

My family lauds my cooking
   From the goodness of their heart—
But they save their crowning comment
   For my choicest works of art.

I puff up like a peacock—
   Let the cook resist who could,
The compliment of compliments—
   "Oh boy, that's lickin' good!"

JULY 14, 1926

Swapping Recipes

(Suggested by Mrs. J. A. T.)

The room is filled with humming,
   Like hives of swarming bees—
The sewing circle's busy
   At swapping recipes!

Miss Jenkins beams, and dictates
   Her cake receipt with pride,
And Mrs. Tucker's flattered
   When questioned by a bride.

For one heart-breaking moment
   I think they scorn my art—
And then they beg the secret
   Of my Banbury tart!

No other entertainment
   Is quite so sure to please,
For a woman's dearest pleasure
   Is swapping recipes!

OCTOBER 30, 1926

The Symphony of Supper-time

I like the sound of silver,
    When the table's being set,
In the early Winter twilight,
    With the lamps unlighted yet.

I like to hear the kitchen door
    Swing slowly out, and then,
When Mary passes, laden, through,
    Swing slowly back again.

I like to hear the kettle sing;
    The hissing of the roast;
The children coming in from play,
    A hungry, noisy host.

I like to hear the murmurings
    When my dessert appears.
The symphony of supper-time
    Is music to my ears!

NOVEMBER 20, 1926

After Dinner

About the table still we sup,
    And laugh and jest and idly chat
And loath to break the circle up,
    We talk of this, we talk of that.

Tomorrow all our ways may go
    Separate, scattered, one by one.
Where it may find us, who can know?
    We cannot see from sun to sun.

But now, and here, and close, we meet,
    Enclosed in friendship's magic charm.
Companionship is dear and sweet;
    And so we linger, arm on arm.

Out of life's vast uncertainty
    This feast of comradeship is spread.
Tomorrow be as it may be—
    Tonight, together, we break bread.

AUGUST 13, 1927

On the Job

(Suggested by B. M. G.)

I can't play cards all afternoon—
My nerves fast wearing thinner—
When I'm expecting company
That very night for dinner.

I cannot seem to plan things right
And have the courses ready.
If I'm not home by five o'clock
I'm nervous and unsteady.

I cannot serve a fancy meal
The days that I hob-nob.
My reputation is at stake—
I must be on the job!

FEBRUARY 13, 1928

The Smell of Country Sausage

I call them twice to breakfast—
    Then, if they are not there,
I let the smell of sausage
    Waft up the kitchen stair.

The smell of country sausage
    Beats any breakfast bell
For routing out the sleepy-heads—
    It means hot cakes as well!

The smell of country sausage
    Drifts in across their dream,
With buckwheat cakes and syrup
    As thick as Jersey cream.

I let the spiced aromas
    Call up the kitchen stair.
Before I have my table set,
    The family all is there!

MAY 24, 1926

Waffle Hunger

(Suggested by Mrs. N. C. H.)

When nights grow cold and frosty,
    Folks grow displeased,
And their rising waffle-hunger
    Must be appeased.

"We're hungry for waffles!"
    Comes the call.
I pour two quarts of batter
    In a pitcher tall.

Then out comes the butter,
    The marmalade jug,
The strained clover honey
    And the maple syrup jug.

Folks eat as many waffles
    As I will bring.
A full-grown waffle-hunger
    Is a terrible thing!

OCTOBER 19, 1926

The Queen's Breakfast

They served the Queen a breakfast dish
   A famous French chef makes,
But from my soul I pity her—
   She had no buckwheat cakes!

Sweetbreads she had, in ramequins,
   And lambs' tongues, broiled and spiced,
And tho' the day was chill, poor soul,
   She had her grapefruit iced.

She does not know the rich delights
   Of maple syrup poured
Over a stack of buckwheat cakes,
   With buttery goodness stored.

Tomorrow's breakfast's in the press.
   She's having mignon steaks,
And grouse-breast à la reine. But ah,
   We're having buckwheat cakes!

NOVEMBER 1, 1926

This Morning's Pancakes

This morning's pancakes were so good
My folks refused all other food.
    The other courses went to waste
    Before the pancakes' perfect taste.

Tom poured the maple syrup thick,
And with appreciative lick
    So scraped and tarried at his plate,
    The school-bell rang, and he was late.

The family cleared a mammoth platter—
I made a second batch of batter.
    Each pancake was ambrosial stuff—
    It seemed they could not get enough.

This most delightful breakfast feat
I am unlikely to repeat.
    And lest I be too much on trial,
    I shan't serve pancakes for a while!

MAY 31, 1927

Ancestral Pies

Great-grandma baked such cherry pies
　　That LaFayette, a guest one night,
Took one to bed in pleased surprise
　　And ate it in the dead of night.

Grandma baked them for the Grange,
　　Apple her best, tho' some said mince.
So, trained from youth, it isn't strange
　　That I've made pastry ever since.

They gather round my floury board,
　　Shades of ancestral cooks, to see
If I betray the art they stored
　　In cook-books handed down to me.

And oh! the times I've stood dismayed
　　With pie crust or meringue forlorn,
And moaned those ancestors and prayed
　　They'd been wild Indians—fed on corn!

MAY 26, 1926

Cherry Pie

Dear Mrs. Rawlings: If your family loves cherry pie as well as mine does, you will certainly write a verse about it. Mrs. Anna S. T.

When breakfast time brings family "words,"
    And choice, long-hoarded insults fly,
I plan my menu to include
    For dinner, a sweet cherry pie!

There's haughty silence with the soup;
    With meat and salad, icy stares.
And then the cherry pie comes in
    And takes the battlers unawares!

No witches' love charm ever worked
    A quicker spell than that sweet dish.
Two helpings—and they try to fill,
    Each one, the other's slightest wish!

I hope they never find me out!
    It's worked so well, I quite rely,
For family-soothing purposes,
    On sweet and juicy cherry pie!

JULY 12, 1926

Lemon Pie

I struggled ten or fifteen years
    To make good lemon pie.
The crust was thin, the paste was thick,
    And the meringue was dry.

The crust was thick, the filling thin,
    The top was limp and flat!
I thought: I've met my Waterloo—
    I'll never master that!

But I toiled on, while bitter tears
    Fell often on my board.
And now I'll draw a peaceful breath—
    I've reaped a rich reward!

I heard the village gossip say,
    Today, as I passed by:
"I never liked her, but she makes
    A perfect lemon pie!"

JULY 23, 1926

Up Against It

(A Tragedy Related by Mrs. A. T. S.)

I told Himself, "You brought this man
    To dinner without any warning.
I'll feed you both as best I can—
    You know I've been away since morning."

"I have one piece of cherry pie,
    Of last night's apple pie, another.
Your guest can choose—then you and I
    Must choose—remember now—the other."

The guest chose apple pie. Himself
    Allowed that cherry'd taste delightful.
We cleared my scanty pastry shelf—
    When on my ear fell phrases frightful:

"I wonder if I might have more"—
    Oh for a pie-producing fairy!—
Our guest asked, "From your generous store
    Might I have now a piece of cherry?"

JANUARY 30, 1928

When Mary Makes Molasses Cake

When Mary makes molasses cake
   We all forget the fact
That she is Perkins' servant girl,
   Of simple speech and act.

The children of the neighborhood
   All flock to Perkins' door.
And even Dr. Smith was heard
   To beg for one piece more!

When spiced and gingered airs announce
   Molasses cake is done,
We all make some excuse to go
   To Perkins', one by one!

Six days a week she's "Perkins' girl,"
   In dingy gingham gown.
But when she makes molasses cake,
   Why, Mary owns the town!

JULY 26, 1926

The Hypocrite

My family is generous
  With thanks for pies and cakes,
They know I stand and make them
  For their dear hungry sakes.

They know I'm always ready
  To stir up gingerbread.
Or shape a cookie-gentleman
  With raisins on his head.

Dessert, today, brought praises
  And smiling gratitude,
Avowals that none other
  Prepares such luscious food.

I was a shameful hypocrite,
  As I took it from the shelf.
The truth is, I got hungry
  For chocolate cake, myself!

APRIL 20, 1927

Home-made Ice Cream

Allow for fifty pounds of ice,
    And half a day of fuss.
Allow for all the cellar floor
    And kitchen, in a muss.

Allow for frenzied, fierce disputes
    On the amount of salt.
Allow for endless "tasting," while
    The freezing has to halt!

Allow for jealousy and tears—
    The dasher's being licked!
Allow for pleas of "Hurry!" when
    The dinner hour is picked.

Be sure to make vast quantities.
    You must allow, 'twould seem,
For simply scandalous appetites
    For real home-made ice cream!

JULY 21, 1926

Spilt Milk

Spilt milk is wasted, every bit—
It's gone, and that's the end of it.
    No tears, no sighs, for what-might-be
    Is my spilt-milk philosophy.

When boys break windows with a ball,
The panes are broken—that is all.
    Accidents happen now and then,
    I've noticed, to some grown-up men.

And if I spoil a cake or pie
I give no loud, heart-broken cry.
    Scorched and ruined apple-sauce
    I charge to profit and to loss.

But I am mourning to this day
The time, when at a picnic gay,
    Through my own stupid, careless fault,
    I got the ice cream full of salt!

JUNE 16, 1927

Prize Jelly

Yes, that's my apple jelly,
   And that's the currant there.
They took first prizes, both of them,
   Up at the County Fair.

Why, no, I don't mind telling
   What makes them sparkle so—
Nothing on earth but sunshine,
   Before they "jell," you know.

Make them the same as always,
   Then put them in the sun.
They drink it in and hold it,
   Sun won't fail anyone.

You know, I think some folks need
   The self-same thing as well—
A long, deep draught of sunshine
   To make their spirits "jell!"

JUNE 2, 1926

The Busiest Woman

(Suggested by Mrs. Frances N—)

"My day's so full," (we were comparing notes)
    One woman said, "I have no time to read."
Another busy mother never votes,
    And told great tales of being rushed indeed.

"I too am busy," smiled a mother then.
    "My time goes, satisfying appetite.
My daily family table numbers ten,
    And they are hungry, morning, noon, and night."

"I can't make jellies by the glass at all.
    I make quince jelly in a three-quart tin,
Plum by the gallon pail. My cellar wall
    Is lined with jam tubs, pickle vats, worn thin."

With one accord, we all arose and bowed,
    And thought, we do not know what full days are.
The busiest woman in the state, we vowed—
    Too rushed to make her jell in glass or jar.

JANUARY 31, 1927

Bread and 'Lasses

Molasses cookies, gingerbread,
   Molasses fudge, molasses cake—
Small tongues are always hanging out,
   When I bring "'lasses" out to bake.

They want "a taste," they want a spoon.
   They're underfoot all baking day.
I give them "bread and 'lasses" then,
   To make them take themselves away!

I see them underneath the trees,
   With sticky hands and blissful smiles.
To get "more 'lasses" they employ
   The most amazing arts and wiles!

Molasses, to their eager taste,
   Should flow from an unending font.

AUGUST 7, 1926

Buckwheat Honey

Some folks prefer the clover brand
    Because it's clear and sunny,
But every time, for taste and smell,
    I'll take dark buckwheat honey!

Because I praise its flavor so,
    I've been considered "funny."
But what, on buckwheat griddle cakes,
    Beats mellow buckwheat honey?

On biscuits, fluffy, brown and crisp,
    It drips, so richly runny!
And what makes cupboards smell as sweet
    As fragrant buckwheat honey?

I wouldn't lose it from my shelves
    For love or fame or money.
Nectar, as far as I'm concerned,
    Is really buckwheat honey!

AUGUST 27, 1926

Cold Turkey

Now some folks like their turkey hot,
    Well-roasted to bronze-gold,
And eaten steaming from the stove;
    But my folks like it cold.

I thought our fat Thanksgiving bird
    Would serve another day;
Our guests devoured it to the bones
    Before they went away!

We're dining out on Christmas Day,
    And not at all enticed.
Because we cannot even hint
    To have cold turkey sliced!

Housewives should please their families,
    Fair means or foul, I hold.
I'll roast a turkey on the sly,
    And serve it to them cold!

DECEMBER 7, 1926

Pleasing Everybody

(Suggested by Mrs. Victor L.)

Pleasing everybody—or trying to!
Wondering whether a meal will "do"—
    This is the housewife's fount of grief—

And that's the trouble with a roast of beef.
Some like it hot and others cold;
Some want it "standing," others, "rolled;"
    Most like it rare, but there's always one
    Who cries to the heavens if it's not well-done.

Down on my knees by the oven-door—
Had I better give it a minute more?
    When it's cooked just right, it's brown of skin,
    Well-done without, but rare within.

When it's being carved, my heart stands still—
Is it too well-done for Uncle Bill?
    The crisis is passed and my breathing's eased—
    The roast's just right, and everybody's pleased!

MARCH 29, 1927

The Last Vegetable

(Suggested by Mrs. G. T. C., Atlanta, Ga.)

If you should come to visit me,
　You might not care to stay,
For okra is our staple food
　At least three times a day!

The long drought finished up my beans;
　The caterpillar dines
On cabbages; the sun dried up
　My fat tomato vines.

Only the lowly okra stands,
　Deserted and alone,
Last on the garden battle-field,
　Its brother-warriors prone!

I serve it fried and baked and stewed.
　Because it's "done its bit"
And stuck to me through thick and thin,
　Why, I shall stick to it!

OCTOBER 7, 1927

Holiday Left-overs

(Suggested by Mrs. A. B. R.)

Nobody ate any onions,
    But the cranberry jell disappeared.
They scarcely touched squash or potatoes,
    But the platter of turkey was cleared.

My pantry with celery and stuffing,
    With left-over dishes, was piled.
But there wasn't a scrap of plum pudding.
    My manner was gentle and mild—

But I sternly served up the left-overs.
    "You gobbled the things you preferred—
Now here is the rest of the dinner,"
    And nobody dared say a word!

DECEMBER 27, 1927

A Meal of Almost Nothing

"It's a meal of almost nothing."
  She said, "just scraps I had."
I saw her ample larder
  And I chuckled, "That's too bad!"

Her odds-and-ends were chicken,
  Fruit, mushrooms, fancy cheese—
Why, I could make a banquet
  Out of odds-and-ends like these!

When I say a meal is gathered
  From a pantry bare and clean,
That it's made of almost nothing,
  That's exactly what I mean!

FEBRUARY 8, 1928

Mothers and Motherhood

To Mother

There is no payment I can make
For those long hours you lay awake
    And helped a baby fight for breath—
    A living bulwark against death.

There are no thanks that I can tend
For sacrifices without end;
    For days and weeks and months and years
    Of comforting my griefs and tears.

There is no gift for you as choice
As the sweet music of your voice;
    No flower, no costly jewel, as rare
    As the dear smile you used to wear.

Then may I bring you, not too late,
The thing you patiently await;
    The stuff your life was molded of,
    The only gift you ask for—love.

MAY 7, 1927

The Jolly Tramp

"Lady, if you will give me food,"
    The jolly hobo said,
"I'll paint your picture in the clouds,
    Tonight when the sun grows red."

"I am an artist from Heav'n," said he,
    With a twinkle in his eye;
And so I fed him buckwheat cakes
    And gingerbread and pie.

A hoe was missing when he went,
    Three silver forks were gone,
The patent sprinkler disappeared
    From off our thirsty lawn.

But that night when the picture-clouds
    Across the west trooped by,
"Oh come and look!" the children called
    "There's mother in the sky!"

MAY 16, 1927

Other Women's Babies

I didn't like to tell her,
   (Poor soul, she was so proud)
That when my Tom was thirteen months
   He said whole words out loud.

She thought it so unusual
   Her baby crept at ten.
My Tom was climbing on the chairs
   And taking long steps then!

Some women have such notions
   About their baby's brain.
I have kept my lips shut
   Time and time again.

Of late, I have said nothing,
   Bound by my resolutions.
I show them Tommy's picture,
   To draw their own conclusions!

MAY 25, 1926

All Boy

He's just "all boy!" I can't expect
   To live like women who have girls.
My house is just about half-wrecked—
   He doesn't throw his things—he hurls!

Tousled and grimy, into everything,
   Freckled, with such a toothless grin!
Cookies and cakes? They just take wing!
   I've worn out my third rolling pin.

Oh that one peaceful day might pass
   Without a bloody nose or knee!
If he'd sit quiet on the grass
   One hour, it would be bliss to me!

But would I change him? Not for pearls!
   His muddy foot-steps bring me joy!
I wouldn't trade him for ten girls—
   I'm sinful proud that he's "all boy!"

MAY 29, 1926

Making the Beds

They will stretch weary in these snowy sheets,
    Tom and the twins and little blue-eyed Sue.
Worn out with play, they'll seek these white retreats
    For deep oblivious slumber. And I, too,

Will be so weary when the day is done
    That drawing breath is pain. There isn't time
For one day's tasks from rushing sun to sun,
    And life is hurried as a gypsy rhyme,

Two sheets for each small bed, two pillow-slips,
    Smooth and fresh-washed, like daisies after rain.
(How the soft moonlight on their faces drips,
    Silvers their fingers on the counter-pane!)

They will sleep here tonight, so let me give
    What time and life conspire to take away:
Slumber made smooth and sweet by hands that live
    Only to love and serve them every day.

JUNE 9, 1926

Loving

Tidying up where toys and games were thrown,
    Where tangled kites in chandeliers were caught,
I sighed to think, "How soon they will be grown!
    Then they will thank me for my love." I thought:

Suppose the day of thanking never comes.
    Suppose their childish love shall run away.
Suppose their hearts on mine shall fail to hum
    With that dear comradeship that fills each day.

Without their love, could I endure to live?
    Would mine be wasted, with their love untrue?
And then, O mothers, you who give—and give—
    My heart leaped up and sang for joy—I knew!

Finer the giving than the gratitude;
    Love's hand's so fair that it should go ungloved.
A woman's serving, her beatitude—
    Richer by far the lover than the loved!

JUNE 10, 1926

The Menagerie

I'm so embarrassed when the pastor calls—
    Our yard, someway, is strangely like a zoo.
On turtles, guinea pigs and mice he falls,
    But when there's room enough, what can I do?

"It's hungry, Mother, and its tail is hurt."
    Am I to teach a child to be unkind?
So into rags we tear another shirt,
    And one more rabbit wears a flag behind!

Pigeons and grass-snakes, newts and water rats,
    Squealing and piping all the long day through;
Three-legged pups and bob-tailed, wild-eyed cats,
    But when there's food enough, what can I do?

Lord, if I go to Heaven, will there be
    Some beast-less nook where I can rest my head?
Or has each cherub his menagerie—
    And must I nurse it after I am dead?

JUNE 11, 1926

Twins

They're twice as much trouble,
    Make twice as much noise—
Young twin bears don't eat as much
    As young twin boys!

Twice as many bowls of milk,
    And pills to coax down.
Twice as many lollipops
    When we go to town.

Twice as many steps to take,
    When the day begins.
I didn't think of holes in socks
    When I prayed for twins!

They're twice the standard mixture
    Of monkey, imp and dove.
There's twice as much small boy to scold—
    But twice as much to love!

JUNE 16, 1926

Baby Sue's Bath

I vow, Sue no more needs a bath
  Than any fresh Killarney rose!
But rub the foamy lather on,
  From golden head to sea-shell toes.

She stretches out her dimpled hands
  To catch the bubbles as they rise.
Each ripple is a miracle,
  Each soapy splash a gay surprise.

Yes, let Aunt Annie watch the fun
  Before we tuck Sue up in bed,
See how the sunlight blues her eyes
  And gilds her water-tousled head!

Now wrap her snugly for her nap,
  In her own loveliness enmeshed.
Her bath does me more good than Sue—
  It always leaves me so refreshed!

JUNE 18, 1926

Picnics

A dozen jars of olives,
   And pickles to your taste,
Another batch of cookies
   To be stirred up in haste!

Fried chicken, ham and "wienies,"
   Chops for the roaring fire.
"No, find your own clean stockings."
   They think I never tire!

Then pile into the flivver—
   Now I can draw a breath.
These wild and merry picnics
   Will drive me to my death!

But when I've passed beyond the pale
   Of antics of this sort,
I want each mad-cap child to think,
   "Say, Mother was a sport!"

JUNE 19, 1926

Footprints

In spring, their muddy footprints
　　Make tracks from door to door;
And all the rains of April
　　Cross my kitchen floor.

In summer and in autumn
　　It's leaves and sticks and grass,
And shoes shed four-leaf clovers
　　Where the twins and Tommy pass.

In winter, snowy puddles
　　Will mark each indoor race—
But still I'll give them cookies,
　　And kiss each frosty face.

For through the round of seasons,
　　With childhood's magic art,
Their well-loved feet are tracing
　　Footprints on my heart.

JUNE 24, 1926

Independence Day

The day will start at sunrise,
  With small boys all about,
Making their preparations
  To turn things inside out!

My kitchen will be littered
  With fireworks, every size,
And I'll spend the day in watching
  That they don't put out their eyes.

I'll turn the whole day over
  To picnic-ing and noise,
To supplying punk and matches
  For half a dozen boys!

The Fourth for me is bedlam,
  Tho' safe and sane for others.
Perhaps some year they'll celebrate
  Independence Day for mothers!

JULY 3, 1926

"The Kids Across the Track"

It's perfectly amazing,
    The harm those children do.
They must be little hoodlums,
    But sly and cautious, too.

They play their pranks—then vanish.
    Their record's very black.
At least, so say the children
    Of "the kids across the track."

I asked my neighbor's Jimmy,
    "Who broke my window-pane?"
"The kids across the track," he beamed,
    "Were over here again!"

Now I have a strange suspicion—
    I may have to take it back—
That they're purely a convenience—
    "The kids across the track!"

JULY 9, 1926

Coxey's Army

I've played a friendly "goody-game"
　　With Tommy and his friends;
A game well-planned, I must confess,
　　For their small stomachs' ends!

If they invent a likely tale,
　　Then I must let them in,
And give them something good to eat.
　　Of course, they always win!

I've fed "the King's own messengers,"
　　"Beggars," "spies" and "scouts."
But whether I can keep it up,
　　I have appalling doubts!

Small boys half filled my yard today!
　　They called as one, "Please, Ma'am.
We're that guy Coxey's Army—
　　And we'd like some bread and jam!"

July 17, 1926

Perch Fishing

(Suggested by C. A.)

Small boys wreck my fernery
    In digging worms for bait.
They get their fishlines tangled
    About the garden gate.

Their "minny-pails" spill over
    On all my nicest rugs.
They leave the back porch covered
    With mangled bits of bugs.

They keep the washtub handy
    To put their perch-strings in,
They come home hot and "fishy,"
    With a delighted grin.

I fry their three-inch fishes,
    As solumn as a church.
And then I risk my soul to say,
    "My, what delicious perch!"

JULY 30, 1926

Always Hungry

My children always say they're "starved."
    You'd think they'd never had enough!
You'd think, when we go into town,
    They'd never seen a whipped cream puff!

They flatten noses, hands and cheeks
    Against the bakers' windowpanes.
When buttered popcorn fills the air,
    They're accurate as weather-vanes!

Mid-morning, middle-afternoon,
    It's "Can't we have a bite to eat?"
To satisfy those appetites
    Would be a superhuman feat!

I sometimes fear that on my grave
    My tombstone will be harshly carved:
"She must have failed her little ones.
    They were always hungry, always starved!"

AUGUST 5, 1926

Hide and Seek

There was a garden, long ago,
    Where children played at hide and seek.
And through a vine-clad Summerhouse
    The hiding players used to peek.

There was an attic, cubby-holed,
    Where half the neighborhood could hide,
With run-ways underneath the eaves,
    Where you could burrow, if you tried.

A younger generation now
    Outside my door is scampering;
And I should like to join their games,
    And enter in their frolicking.

Watching, I think of games once played—
    So long, and still it seems last week!
For if the heart is young, one feels
    Never too old for hide and seek!

AUGUST 11, 1926

Grandma's Chair

This used to be her favorite chair,
　And here she sat with folded hands;
And on her hair, so smooth and white,
　A lace cap lay, with ribbon bands.

She used to rock, and hold the cat,
　Purring in her aproned lap;
And here, when no one looked her way,
　She nodded in a hasty nap.

She used to read her favorite book,
　And do some knitting now and then,
Until her spectacles slipped off,
　And Grandma was asleep again.

Somehow, I seldom sit in it;
　I seem to see her drowsing there.
I like to keep the cushion smoothed;
　It still, to me, is Grandma's chair.

AUGUST 20, 1926

Burning the Grass

(Suggested by J. H. R.)

All up and down the village
    The boys, fast bustling, pass,
With torches, brooms and buckets
    To burn the meadow grass.

All Summer they've avoided
    Much honest, needed work.
Lawn-mowing and grass-trimming
    They've tried their best to shirk.

But now, with righteous faces,
    They're burning grass and weeds
Preventing propagation,
    They claim, of thistle seeds.

Now I wouldn't play the cynic,
    Or rouse their injured ire—
But is this grown-up industry—
    Or a small-boy love of fire?

SEPTEMBER 25, 1926

Worrying

Someday I shall be very wise,
    And I shall know that night-time brings
A weary body and weary mind
    That let in hordes of worryings.

Some day, I think, I'll know enough
    To close my eyes at night in sleep,
Not let one goblin care come near,
    Or let one impish worry peep!

Now, did I over-scold the twins?
    Should I have sent poor Tom to bed?
(Three spankings would have done no harm!)
    Who'd bring them up if I were dead?

And then when morning sparkles in,
    When sun and blue sky gleam without,
I can't think for the life of me,
    What I was worrying so about!

NOVEMBER 5, 1926

Family Quarrels

Folks can't live together
Without some stormy weather.
   Everybody, every day,
   Gets in another's way.

"Birds in their nest agree"—
But somehow, it seems to me,
   Soft notes alone are heard
   From a rather stupid bird.

Families longing to be clever
Claim they never squabble, never.
   They may speak as smooth as butter,
   I don't believe a word they utter!

Quarrels but sweeten friendship's cup—
It's so pleasant making up.
   Sun follows tempest everywhere—
   Family storms clear up the air!

NOVEMBER 29, 1926

Old Doctor Parker

Old Doctor Parker,
    With his shabby grip,
Is coming up the pathway,
    With his agile old trip.

There's "pep'mint" in his pocket,
    And the convalescent twins
Will listen to his funny tales,
    All chuckles and grins.

Couldn't trust his hand, of course,
    With a crisis near—
But children trust his kindly heart,
    And love his jolly cheer.

Old Doctor Parker's calls
    Are worth a box of pills.
Sunshine's recommended,
    I think, for children's ills!

JANUARY 17, 1927

No School

"No school!" There won't be any books for months!
    No teachers and no lessons and no sums!
But there'll be kittens, and new puppies, too;
    And just-hatched wrens, to feed and tame with crumbs.

No books! But there'll be boats to build and sail,
    The lake's a volume in biology,
And full of fishes and strange weeds and shells.
    And all their games will teach philosophy!

No lessons! But they somehow learn that trees
    Are kindly, after playing in the sun.
They find there's fun in sharing picnic food!
    They find that rest is sweet, when romping's done.

No teachers! But they figure out the law
    That nature first is harsh—and then is kind.
Happy, contented, they will quickly learn
    A friendly world awaits a friendly mind.

JUNE 29, 1926

Dressing for School

(Suggested by Mrs. Muriel E. E.)

Now, bless me, only yesterday
I know I put clean shirts away,
    But Tommy, dressing on the run,
    Declares there's not a single one.

The twins are dawdling with their socks,
Oblivious of the speeding clocks—
    And then there'll be a tumbling rush
    To grab the toothpaste, comb and brush!

The cocoa and the toast grow cold,
The warning bell just now has tolled—
    And there's a maudlin scrambling 'round,
    With schoolbooks nowhere to be found!

No words of reprimand avail,
All modes of disciplining fail;
    It's natural to make a stew
    Of what one does not want to do!

JANUARY 28, 1927

The Bottomless Pit

No one seems to know
 Where it is found.
Is it where demons go,
 Underground?

Is it eternity—
 The furthest night—
In which whole worlds may be
 Out of sight?

No, I have found the truth!
 I offer here
My answer, and, forsooth,
 My fear.

I've recognized, with awe,
 The bottomless pit.
A small boy's empty maw—
 That's it!

APRIL 6, 1927

Bedlam

The twins have two dogs
    And a cross old cat—
And I sometimes don't know
    Where I am "at!"

Tom has a parrot
    With an evil beak—
And it nips the cat's tail
    Twice a week.

The boys and the animals
    Shriek and race,
'Til there's riotous bedlam
    All over the place.

If patient mothers
    Cared to speak,
They'd start a "Be-Kind-
    To-Housewives-Week!"

JUNE 9, 1927

Safe and Sane

There's no such thing as too much noise
Upon the Fourth, for little boys.
    But when the fireworks have begun,
    The dogs turn tail in flight, and run.

There's no such thought for boys as risk,
When Roman candles flare and whisk.
    But mothers shake with fear, despair,
    When giant "crackers" split the air.

Tom is convinced that his best friends
Have cheated him to gain their ends.
    They've made the Fourth—he sees it plain—
    For Fido, safe, for Mother, sane!

Small boys have broken hearts today
Who aren't allowed explosive play.
    But dogs are barking with delight.
    Mothers will get some sleep tonight!

JULY 2, 1927

Hoodlums

Tom and the twins are a constant disgrace,
Tattered of breeches and dirty of face;
   Tardy for breakfast and into bed late.
   "You're going to be hoodlums," I say, "sure as fate."

Into the swimming hole, tho' it's forbidden;
Hunting out cookies and cakes that I've hidden;
   Into the buns and the doughnuts and jam—
   I'm sure they'll be hoodlums, I certainly am.

"Hoodlums are willful," I tell them, "and wild.
A hoodlum's a greedy and impudent child,
   Who slams all the screen doors and talks in a shout,
   And that's what you'll be if you aren't watching out."

I paint a grim picture of boys who become
The sort all good people turn horrified from.
   Aren't they disturbed that it may be their lot
   Some day to be hoodlums? Apparently not!

JULY 5, 1927

Almost

Some days I'd almost gladly flee
    Where I could never, never hear
The children's voices calling me,
    Their squabbles ringing in my ear.

When dinner dishes by the score
    Await me from the previous night,
I'd almost throw them out the door,
    Pack up my bag and take to flight.

I've threatened more than once to run,
    When I've been grossly disobeyed,
When I find errands still undone,
    Because Tom dallied, swam or played.

"And would you go?" the children say,
    Solemn before my idle boast.
"And would you really run away?"
    I smile and hug them. "Ah—almost!"

AUGUST 10, 1927

Belief

I don't believe in fairies,
    Goblins, elves or gnomes.
I can't quite think that tiny sprites
    In lilies make their homes.

Time crumbles down the giant,
    Age kills the fairy prince.
I saw an elf when I was five—
    And haven't seen one since!

But somehow, when the children come
    And kneel beside my knee
And listen to a fairy tale
    Wide-eyed with ecstasy,

My cynicism seems to fail!
    I'd scarcely feel surprise
To see a Brownie on the hearth—
    For I'm seeing through their eyes!

AUGUST 27, 1927

The Queen of Hearts

Mother wears no satin gown
    To grace her baking-hour;
Upon her brow no golden crown,
    But a smudge of pastry flour!

No Russian sables wrap her form,
    And yet she holds high court
When from the oven, spiced and warm,
    She takes a fresh date torte.

She never gives a harsh command,
    For hers are gentler arts.
She rules us with a loving hand—
    She is the Queen of Hearts!

SEPTEMBER 24, 1927

Important! Rush!

Who ever began the fiction
    Of childhood's light-hearted joys?
Why, bless me, they're so serious,
    These grave little girls and boys!

They're solemn over their parties;
    They "must" wear this or that;
There's a tragic need of hurry
    In finding a shoe or hat.

When they rush in, begging for cookies,
    Tousled and out of breath,
It's not an occasion for jest—
    It's a matter of life and death!

OCTOBER 5, 1927

The Folks Who'll Feed a Fellow

The world is not divided
   By its sorrow or its joy,
But according as to whether
   It'll feed a hungry boy!

When a fellow comes from calling
   On his grandma or his aunts,
He likes to tuck some cookies
   In the pockets of his pants.

Can he help it if he's hungry?
   Not to offer things is cruel.
Why, he'd starve without a little bite
   Of something after school!

Yes, the world is well divided
   Into those who do or don't:
The folks who'll feed a fellow,
   And the stingy folks who won't!

OCTOBER 8, 1927

Every-day Babies

(Suggested by Mrs. B. L. C.)

Blonde babies? I can't recommend them—
I don't see why the stork must send them.
They're pink and white and cuddly and tickly,
But mercy me, they soil so quickly!

They show the mud from every puddle,
And keep their daintiness all a-muddle.
To let them crawl is an error tactical—
Blonde babies simply are not practical!

Now brunette babies show the dirt less,
Even when they've strayed off, shirtless!
Order them dark, for every-day action—
They give the soundest satisfaction!

DECEMBER 6, 1927

Swearing Off

My family—every one's a glutton—
Stuffed through the holidays on mutton,
On turkey, goose and chicken, too,
And with the new year, cried, "We're through!"

Tom's sworn off puddings, game and pie;
The twins will let all sweets pass by;
Aunt Nellie's through with nuts, she said,
And Uncle Bill with fancy bread.

The New Year finds them virtuous,
From too rich foods, abstemious.
That's fine—of course they do not need them—
But what on earth am I to feed them!

JANUARY 6, 1928

Itching for a Spanking

Tom's itching for a spanking,
    I know the signs too well.
For every inch I give him
    The rascal takes an ell.

I don't believe in spankings—
    I'd spare him if I could—
And yet the imp confessed to me
    "I think they do me good."

He reaches heights of deviltry,
    He disobeys with mirth;
And a good old-fashioned spanking
    Seems to bring him down to earth.

He's pulled the cat's tail, watching me
    With a most hopeful grin.
He's itching for a spanking
    And I might as well give in!

JANUARY 26, 1928

My Children

My children are not mine. I do not own
    Their small, dear bodies, least of all, their souls.
Powers past my powers have built them, flesh and bone.
    Mine but to pilot through life's earlier shoals.

I am the earth; I do not own the flower.
    I am the tree; the fruit I do not own.
Mine but to love these new lives for the hour,
    Not too possessively. They are Time's loan.

I know so little. I can only teach
    The simpler truths that man has learned to trust;
Help them to gracious ways of thought and speech,
    Then let them go their way; for go they must.

FEBRUARY 3, 1928

Domesticity and the Domestic

A Busy Day

(Suggested by Mrs. Ida T—, Louisville, Ky.)

How can a busy housewife ever hope
   For restful days, while always on the run!
It isn't right to be so very tired,
   To be so weary when the day is done.

So thinking, I arranged a whole day "off."
   A day to spend among the trees and birds.
And down a hidden, quiet path, alone,
   I fled for peace from human sounds and words.

I watched the chipmunks and I followed squirrels.
   I helped a moth creep from its damp cocoon.
I tried to find a treetoad when he hummed.
   I listened, breathless, to the crickets' tune.

So free, I should have been as good as new!
   I should have rested there, without a doubt.
Can Life, itself, then, be so strenuous?
   When night came, bless me, I was all tired out!

AUGUST 26, 1926

A Prayer for Housewives

Let me have endless patience, first of all,
   And not grow angry when the quick doors slam,
Or when small fingers stain the new-washed wall.
   Let me ignore the mud tracked o'er the jamb!

Let me be tireless, for the hours are long.
   Let me be merry, when I want to weep.
And if my days may not move like a song,
   Grant me, at night, the healing touch of sleep.

May I remember small, important things—
   An empty cookie jar is such a crime!
Is it too much to pray at times for wings?
   How else, some days, to have the meals on time!

And if there's any fun to come my way,
   Or any laughter due me, Lord, decree it!
And where there's beauty in the every-day,
   Oh, let me not be blinded! Let me see it!

AUGUST 31, 1926

A Mute Housewife

Her language stumbles, and she has no tongue
    To tell her loved ones they are dear as life;
She crooned no lullabies when they were young—
    Mute, as a mother, always, and as wife.

Words do not come to her to say the things
    With which her heart is bursting night and day.
Her love's a captive bird that has no wings,
    Chained by the thoughts it has—and cannot say.

But when she tucks her small ones in at night,
    Or mends their clothes, or irons their sheets with care,
Her face is radiant with a shining light,
    And love, made visible, is present there.

Worn are her knotted fingers. All may see
    The seams and wrinkles made by toil's demands.
Once when I stared at them she smiled at me.
    "I speak my love," she faltered, "with my hands."

JULY 7, 1927

A Housewife's Luxuries

It is my pleasure every day
   To set the table leisurely,
With china patterned bright and gay,
   With silver and fine napery.

My fingers and my eyes delight
   To place pink roses in a bowl,
Arranging them exactly right,
   A treat for any artist's soul.

How I enjoy the evening hours
   When twilight lies across the lawn,
Puttering with my shrubs and flowers
   Before the last pale light is gone.

Bright moments in the every-day,
   These pleasures of a busy wife
Make up for many an hour of gray—
   The daily luxuries of life.

AUGUST 20, 1927

The Chatelaine

I think I should have liked to be
    A mediaeval chatelaine,
With every massive castle key
    Hung on one great important chain.

The chain about my ample waist,
    I'd pass through dungeon, hall and tower;
Inspect the banquet-foods, and taste;
    Unlock vast stores of meal and flour.

Think of the hand-made linens stored
    Upon a man-high, oaken shelf!
The candle-lit huge festal board,
    Laid for an army, by myself!

How grandiose was that distant day,
    When housewives did prodigious feats!
Ah—I must go and put away
    My half-a-dozen cotton sheets!

OCTOBER 4, 1927

It Isn't Work

It isn't work, if you like to do it.
　　It isn't work if it gives a thrill,
If always pleasant thoughts imbue it,
　　If you do it gladly and with a will.

It isn't "housework"—dusting, mending,
　　Scrubbing floors and baking things,
Washing dishes and pans unending,
　　To one who laughs and smiles and sings.

It isn't work, if you find good measure
　　Of cheer and sun in every minute.
It isn't housework—it's home pleasure,
　　With a little love and laughter in it!

NOVEMBER 12, 1927

The Lucky Housewife

Dame Nature stops work in the Fall
And doesn't tidy things at all.
    She calmly passes
    And leaves dead grasses
And wind-swept dust by every wall.

Then on some winter's morning—snow,
Falling thick and soft and slow!
    Her floors neglected,
    As she'd expected,
White-carpeted, no longer show!

Alas, when I leave my debris
Strewn up and down for all to see,
    No miracles hover,
    My sins to cover
And hide my carelessness for me!

JANUARY 7, 1928

A Housewife's Hands

What gave my hands their housewife's skill,
    Their handy way with mop and broom,
Their knack of nursing old and ill,
    Their swiftness tidying up a room?

Whence came the ease with which they dress
    An eager child for school or play,
Or make small beds with soft caress,
    And sketch the order of the day?

Not so much practice o'er and o'er,
    But that the eternal housewife stands
Behind me—those who went before
    With age-old, quick, maternal hands.

FEBRUARY 7, 1928

The Housewife's Heaven

Just enough dust on the golden stair,
   Blown by a breeze from the pearly street,
To keep her a little bit busy there,
   Making her corner of Paradise neat.

Just enough cherubs' small breeches to mend,
   Just enough feathers from angel-wings loose,
Just enough archangel wants to attend,
   To keep her quick, capable fingers in use.

A world full of love to remind her of home,
   With a "spat," for the good of her soul, now and then,
And oh, the vast markets of Heaven to comb
   For foods to delight cherubs, angels and men!

FEBRUARY 27, 1928

Sportsmen's Wives

The golfer's wife, poor thing, poor thing,
Puts up with almost everything.
 Her meals are scorched, warmed-over, late,
 And served to language profligate.

The motorist's wife, poor hurried thing,
Spends all the Summer on the wing.
 She counts that moment sweet and blest
 When punctured tires enforce a rest.

The sailor's wife lives all alone,
And picks a solitary bone.
 She would embrace the chance, poor thing,
 To put up with 'most anything!

JUNE 11, 1927

Mistress and House

A gracious mistress for this gracious place,
　　She moves in harmony with flowers and birds;
　　Her voice is gentle, filled with gentle words
And there is sunlight on her quiet face.

The rooms are sunny, and the light streams here
　　From morn to night. Outside the windows, trees
　　Murmur the year 'round in the soft sweet breeze.
How much is mistress? How much—atmosphere?

Here is a combination choice and good:
　　This lovely home behind its welcoming gate
　　Has found in her its mistress and its mate;
She crowns its beauty with her womanhood.

JANUARY 12, 1928

Houses

Some houses fill me with a strange delight:
    Houses that stand aloof upon a hill,
Looming like castles in the stormy night—
    So bitter-proud, so haughty—and so still.

I have known houses on a lonely road,
    Sunk like dead eyes within a grove of pine,
Where only night-hawks keep their dark abode,
    And bats infest the honeysuckle vine.

Houses of mystery and pride and gloom,
    You stir my mind to swift imaginings.
But oh, make way within my heart! Make room
    For that which gives my tingling spirit wings:

A little house tucked down a cozy lane,
    Rosy within, where logs are burning red;
A candle gleaming through the window-pane,
    Where one sits listening for a loved one's tread.

JUNE 12, 1926

Smell of Old Houses

What makes old houses smell so spicy sweet?
    Haven't you noticed, even at the door,
No matter how fresh-painted or how neat,
    An odor stirs of dainties gone before?

Honey long-stored in cupboards tightly closed
    Leaves perfumed traces in the very walls,
And years of shelves where currant tarts reposed
    Scatter an ancient savour through the halls.

There is a hint of potted pigeon pie,
    Rich pastry odors haunt the deep flour bin;
All the choice luxuries of days gone by
    Have left their spirits on the shelves within.

And, adding fragrance as of potpourri
    Where secret, rare aromas blend and meet,
The ghosts of olden loves breathe constantly.
    That's why old houses smell so spicy sweet.

JUNE 15, 1926

"For Rent"

Such a nice, careless house, just made for boys!
    Two steps are gone, a door hangs by a thread,
On windy nights the shutters make a noise
    Certain to wake the soundest-sleeping dead.

But there's a garden and an apple tree,
    With branches bent into such natural swings!
And there's a barn—it has a loft, you see,
    And there's an attic full of—ghosts and things!

So long so empty and unloved! "For Rent!"
    Across the road it winks a friendly eye,
A house for boisterous mirth and fun just meant—
    And all the prideful mothers pass it by.

But some day, sure, a mother gay will come
    And hear its heart speak. Then, aburst with noise,
Attic and barn and loft with life will hum.
    Such a kind, happy house—just made for boys!

JULY 2, 1926

Candle-light

In daylight, my small shingled house
    Is modest, humble, poor and old,
Shabby beneath the gracious vines
    That shelter it from wind and cold.

The sun strikes in my living-room,
    And shows the carpets, worn and thin,
The fading paper on the walls,
    The curtains held by patch and pin.

But when the chilly daylight goes,
    And tall, slim candles are alight,
The shabbiness just slips away,
    And all my dingy rooms are bright.

My weather-beaten cottage glows,
    And strangers passing by at night
Might sigh: "Oh happy little house,
    Where people live by candle-light!"

JULY 10, 1926

White Houses

A red house, a gray house,
  A house of yellow blind—
None of these can touch my heart,
  Or stir my inmost mind.

A green house, a brown house—
  Folks paint them varied hues.
But a white house hung with creeping vines,
  Is the one I always choose.

Grandmother had a white house;
  My mother lived in one.
And martins twittered in the eaves
  Each day at set of sun.

My hands go out to all I see,
  On every road I roam,
And tuck them in my welcoming heart—
  For each white house is "Home."

NOVEMBER 19, 1926

A Full House

This truth is known to man and wife,
To poker-players in their strife—
A law of poker—and of life:
    A full house beats a pair!

Let quiet, childless homes rejoice
At their sedate and stupid choice;
There's music in a gay young voice:
    A full house beats a pair!

No peace and calm can quite make up
For a jolly crowd drawn close to sup,
For the precious family loving-cup.
    A full house beats a pair!

FEBRUARY 4, 1928

The Kitchen Rocking Chair

The modern cooks make fun of me,
    They like their kitchens white and bare,
While I admit a weakness for
    A cushioned kitchen rocking chair!

I like a red geranium
    Perched on the sunniest window sill,
An ancient and decrepit clock,
    Ticking when all the house is still.

And oh, the comfort when my tasks
    Begin to fret me and to wear,
To sit and do my thinking in
    A cushioned kitchen rocking chair!

For somehow, when I sit me down
    Within its friendly, gay embrace,
Life's petty worries, care and pain
    Are rocked into their proper place!

MAY 27, 1926

The Kitchen Window

Before my kitchen window pass
    The children, laughing, having fun.
I look up from my work and see
    Their games of "Tag" or "Run Sheep Run."

I see the neighbors going by;
    They wave, or call a friendly word.
All up and down the winding road
    Their voices and their steps are heard.

A garden and an apple tree
    Lie in my kitchen window's view;
And every morning, honey-bees
    Visit the roses, wet with dew.

What further could a window hold?
    Not if it framed the earth's two ends
Could there be a wider view than this:
    Laughter and beauty, life and friends!

JULY 19, 1926

Last Night's Dishes

(Suggested by Mrs. Mary L.)

I don't mind letting mending go,
　　Or undarned stockings, deeply piled.
I'm far behind on shirts, I know.
　　But last night's dishes drive me wild!

I don't mind ironing left around
　　A day or two, perhaps a week.
But when last evening's plates abound,
　　The kitchen and the day dawn bleak!

I put off washing window-panes
　　Until there comes a sunny day.
And if it snows or hails or rains,
　　I'm just that much ahead, I say.

I face the morning with a smile
　　With any of these tasks to do.
But dishes that have stood a while?
　　My disposition's Waterloo!

MARCH 4, 1927

The Noisy Kitchen

(Suggested by Mrs. G. H. S.)

I'm noisy in the kitchen.
   I open up my cans
With bangs and bumps and knockings.
   I rattle pots and pans.

I click the kitchen china,
   I thump my rolling pin,
And in my pantry cupboards
   I make a fearful din.

I turn the Dover beater
   With a whole-souled clack and whirr.
I make a glorious racket
   Of anything I stir.

My hungry family tells me
   My noises do not matter.
As signs of coming food, they seem
   A most delightful clatter!

MARCH 12, 1927

Pots and Pans

(Suggested by Elsie Y.)

Pots and pans and kettles!
   I spend so many hours
Scrubbing them and scouring
   The stacks of them, the towers!

Cookie plate and cake-pan,
   Griddle, baking-dish!
To serve from troughs or earthen pots
   Is my irreverent wish!

But ah, without the pie-tin
   No cook could make a pie!
The absence of my gem-pans
   Would leave me high and dry!

I must admit their value
   In cooking, I'm afraid.
Just hand me that unlaundered pile—
   The tools, please, of my trade!

SEPTEMBER 21, 1926

My Cook Stove

(Suggested by Pamelia H.)

You are my black slave, humble, low,
    Who meakly lives to serve my ends.
I learned to trust you long ago,
    To count you with my household friends.

You are the power behind my throne,
    Collaborator in my art;
You have a technique all your own
    In handling cookie, cake or tart.

I take the credit; yours, the pains,
    When pie emerged, crisp and brown.
Because you're faithful, mine the gains
    In cookery prestige through the town.

I shine your worn old honest face.
    With gratitude your needs attend.
We've weathered storms, we've won our race;
    We've stuck together. Hail—my friend!

APRIL 25, 1927

Spring Cleaning

What awful urge is this, that drives
Both tidy and untidy wives
   To clean up almost everything
   And turn things inside out in Spring?

All Winter long I didn't mind
My dusty draperies. Now I find
   I burn to take my curtains down,
   And do the whole affair up brown.

A fearful frenzy seizes me
To go on a housecleaning spree,
   Nor rest 'til everything in sight
   Is cleaned and scrubbed and polished bright.

MARCH 24, 1927

The First Spring Sunshine

(Suggested by Mrs. P. B., Rochester, N.Y.)

The first spring sunshine warms my heart,
　　To see it touch my garden seeds.
It also touches windowpanes
　　And brings to light spring cleaning needs!

It shows the first faint green of grass,
　　It shows the willow buds that swell;
And it shows curtains streaked with grime
　　And rugs in need of soap, as well!

It points to every speck of dust,
　　Suggesting toil laborious.
The first spring sunshine sometimes seems
　　A blessing highly dubious!

February 29, 1928

Cleaning the Attic

(Suggested by Mrs. N. C. H., Westminster Road)

I open little leather trunks,
  Strange ancient boxes, thick with dust.
And there's my mother's wedding dress;
  There's Grand-dad's flint-lock, rough with rust.

The dim and mellow attic light
  Caresses great-grandmother's shawl.
And there are small, dead babies' things,
  A cradle, never used at all.

Love letters, sweet with lavender;
  A wooden doll; a trundle bed;
Daguerreotypes; a whale-oil lamp
  By which forgotten sires had read.

I tip-toe out, the dust untouched.
  Dear faces, voices, hands are near.
I'll have to clean the attic out
  Some other year—some other year.

JULY 22, 1926

Rain on the Roof

I have a room beneath the roof,
   And it is filled with witchery,
When like soft, tapping visitors,
   The raindrops patter over me.

I hear the trees on stormy nights
   Brushing the shingles with their leaves,
And in the after-calm I hear
   The soft rain dripping on the eaves.

I hear the apples strike and bounce,
   I hear the snow fall, and the sleet,
And when it's very still I hear
   A robin's tiny ticking feet.

I get in touch with clouds and sky,
   In that small attic room aloof,
Close to the quiet heart of things,
   With raindrops pattering on the roof.

SEPTEMBER 27, 1926

Memory's Attic

Memory, like an attic, holds
  Such strange, assorted things,
With perfume in their faded folds,
  Or ancient dust that clings.

Such boxes and such books are there,
  Such bundles, put away
In memory's safe and moth-balled air
  Until a later day.

People and places, homes and friends;
  Gardens and trees and flowers;
Beginnings of loves and hates—and ends;
  A lifetime's suns and showers.

I take them out, each one apart,
  From memory's attic. Then,
Refreshed in spirit, mind and heart—
  I put them back again.

MARCH 5, 1927

Darning the Socks

My Dear Mrs. Rawlings: As the paper has extended an invitation to housewives to send in any subjects they wish "glorified," I wish to submit one—not my pet activity by any means, in fact it is one that I detest. Won't you please, kind lady, glorify it for us all—darning the family socks. Mrs. Ella R. B. E.

When I have "staying" company,
    The kind who calls—and stays—and rocks—
I call down blessings on her head—
    For then I darn the family socks!

Two weeks or three, the undarned pile
    Mounts up into a monstrous size,
Until I pass my mending box
    With shamed and half-averted eyes.

But just as tragedy seems near,
    And socks wear perilously thin,
I have a painless darning day,
    For some long-staying guest drops in!

And Nancy Jenks could never guess
    Why at my door she's welcomed so;
I get a whole month's darning done
    Before she says, "Well, I must go!"

JULY 27, 1926

Mending

Dear Mrs. Rawlings: I love to do embroidering, but hate to mend and sew. Now if I could only use bright colors in my mending! Sometime maybe you will write a poem for me. Mrs. George D.

When underwear is frayed and thin,
　　When shirts are tattered, ripped and torn,
I long to throw them quite away—
　　My interest in them, too, is worn!

For after I have patched the pants,
　　Turned the shirt-cuffs, darned the socks,
I've only filled in vacancies,
　　And emptied one more mending box!

The reason I rebel, I think,
　　Is that my mending doesn't show!
If I could darn with bright red silk,
　　I'd not begrudge the time, I know!

Some desperate, frenzied mending day,
　　I'll darn with reds and blues, full tilt;
Deck my astonished family out,
　　All looking like a patchwork quilt!

AUGUST 9, 1926

Washings on the Line

I've studied all my neighbors,
    From their washings on the line.
Their linens, socks and shirts have been
    Often a tell-tale sign!

The fashionable Miss Spenser
    Wears many a torn chemise.
Our high-toned doctor's underwear
    Needs patching at the knees!

As I hung out my wash today,
    I noticed that my sheets
Were ragged, and that Tommy's pants
    Were sadly minus seats.

It dawned on me in horror—
    As for washings on the line,
While I've been studying neighbors',
    Neighbors have studied mine!

AUGUST 14, 1926

Canning

(Suggested by Mrs. B—)

The air is filled with goodness,
    With sugar and with spice,
With syrupy aromas
    Of everything that's nice.

Like flies, the children cluster,
    To scrape the jelly pan.
The whole town's canning cherries,
    To cheer the inner man!

The neighbors go a-borrowing
    For sugar, cinnamon;
They find they're short of rubbers,
    When the preserves are done!

And when the hub-bub's over,
    Smug satisfaction reigns.
A cellar full of good things
    Is worth a Summer's pains!

AUGUST 17, 1926

Dusting

(Requested by Mrs. Maud M. A.)

The dust upon my table,
   The dust upon my chairs,
Is blown in from the highway,
   Where all the great world fares.

I need to dust each morning,
   To keep my small house neat,
And I am often wearied
   By all those passing feet.

But where a house is dustless,
   That house is lone and chill,
And no one ever passes,
   And the road is always still.

So as I do my dusting,
   I think, Why should I sigh?
A dusty house is friendly,
   For folks are going by!

AUGUST 24, 1926

No System

(Suggested by Mrs. S. Alice B.)

I have no system in my house.
    No "ironing day" is mine.
I bake when pantry shelves grow lean,
    I wash when days are fine.

"Wash on Monday, iron on Tuesday,
    Wednesday you must mend"—
Grandma's "system" filled the week,
    But left no time to spend!

"Market Thursday, clean on Friday,
    Bake on Saturday"—
There is no room for ease or friends,
    When life is lived this way!

Life's sweeter when it holds the taste
    Of unexpectedness.
"No system!" is the door
    That lets in happiness.

NOVEMBER 26, 1926

Excuses

I do not seem to clean my house
    At quite the proper seasons.
But no one dares to call me down—
    I find such splendid reasons!

It isn't nice to discommode
    One's household guests, now is it?
How could I turn things inside out
    When friends were here to visit!

Invincible my alibis
    For duties left unfinished,
For unswept rooms, neglected dust
    And brasses long unburnished.

The head should save the heels, they say.
    The saying has its uses.
When I neglect my household tasks
    I have the best excuses!

FEBRUARY 23, 1927

Interruptions

When I sit down with my mending,
　　The puss jumps in my lap,
And curls up on the stockings
　　To take a little nap.

The twins climb up in the evening
　　As I'm answering my mail,
And tease for a game or a romping
　　Or a rousing pirate tale.

Friends drop in when I'm cleaning,
　　Or struggling to trim a hat,
And I must stop my working
　　To gossip with them and chat.

These hindrances and distractions,
　　Strangely, do not irk—
Such friendly interruptions
　　Are pleasanter than work!

APRIL 21, 1927

Neighbors

I don't pretend to love them all—
    Miss Perkins is a fearful cat—
But when the baby had the croup
    She brought me up her best goose-fat.

The doctor's wife is quite a snob—
    She sniffs when I hang out the clothes.
But when I lay so darkly ill
    She brought me her first Russell rose.

Miss Smith complains about my boys.
    She thinks I should have drowned the twins.
But, bringing broth when they had mumps,
    She said, "Oh, well, all boys have sins."

I don't pretend to love them all—
    But when my household is distressed
They're kinder far to me than yours—
    And so I like my neighbors best!

JUNE 17, 1926

A Neighbor's Duties

A friendly soul has just moved near,
    Within our neighborhood.
"What are my duties, please?" she asked.
    "I want my standing good!"

A neighbor's duties should include
    The loan of salt and flour!
The taking in of a neighbor's wash,
    When threatened by a shower.

A neighbor should be helpful,
    And ease her neighbor's cares,
Up to a certain point—then she
    Should mind her own affairs!

The Golden Rule's the teacher
    In any neighbor's school.
I sometimes think that neighbors
    First formed the Golden Rule!

SEPTEMBER 10, 1926

A Snippy Neighbor

I know she privately looks down
Upon my gingham morning-gown,
That plain but most expedient frock.
She's dressed in silk at nine o'clock.

She cannot understand my joy
In feeding some small hungry boy.
She doesn't like the noise they make,
The half-starved way boys gobble cake!

She doesn't like my homely ways,
The gay disorder of my days,
The way our household jokes and sings.
She's far above such common things.

But when it comes to help with pies,
She hangs around, and hints, and sighs.
And when she needs a recipe,
She's glad enough to smile at me!

SEPTEMBER 16, 1927

Old-Fashioned Neighbors

Old-fashioned neighbors just run in
    Next door, to pass the time of day.
    They say, "I'm busy, I can't stay,"
But they'll sit down, if urged, and "chin."

Old-fashioned neighbors bake a pie
    And bring a whole half in to you.
    There's nothing that they wouldn't do
With trouble or with sickness nigh.

An old-time neighbor's scarce, I know—
    Helpful, unenvious, kindly, good.
    If one lives in your neighborhood,
Hang on to her—don't let her go!

FEBRUARY 1, 1928

The Back Door

"Company" comes to the front door
  And knocks politely there.
But friends run in at the back door
  As "company" wouldn't dare.

The children come in the back door,
  Hungry, noisy and gay;
And neighbors' kindness enters
  A dozen times a day.

The front door has a knocker,
  A lock, a bolt and a bell,
But the back door's always open,
  And both doors serve me well.

For houses have always had two doors,
  Since hearts and homes have been,
And the front door keeps the world out—
  And the back door lets it in.

JUNE 26, 1926

When Company Helps

(Suggested by E. W. K., New York City)

When company helps with the dishes
    We visit and dawdle along—
And I find my pans mixed in the cupboards
    And all of my dishes piled wrong.

When company helps with the cooking
    We gossip, we laugh and we chat—
And neglected roasts scorch in the oven
    And souffles, forgotten, grow flat.

When company helps with the cleaning
    Talk flies—not the dirt—in the room;
For with tongues wagging faster than dusters,
    There's more conversation than broom.

Intentions are good and are honest.
    They mean to be helpful, no doubt.
But the one way to get things accomplished
    Is to lock all the company out!

MAY 20, 1927

Company's Coming!

Company's coming! Uncle Lou,
Aunt Em and seven cousins, too.
    We've got four beds and the attic leaks,
    But say, we hope they'll stay six weeks!

Company's coming! Make a cake
Stuffed full of fruits and nuts, and bake
    Several yards of gingerbread
    For Bill and Jim and Tom and Ed!

Bring the ice-cream freezer up
And find the old salt-measure cup.
    Make sure the dasher's turning right.
    Company has such an appetite!

Turn the whole house upside-down—
Company's coming from out of town.
    Load the table till it creaks,
    For, say, we hope they'll stay six weeks!

AUGUST 19, 1927

A Thoughtless Hostess

I thought my technique perfect
   In caring for a guest;
I piled fat feather pillows
   Upon her bed, for rest.

I served her breakfast coffee
   Afloat with golden cream;
But my kindnesses I'm finding
   Less kindly than they seem!

She would have liked small pillows
   For large ones tire her back;
My thick cream just distresssed her—
   She takes her coffee black!

Her tastes were not consulted.
   Cream, pillows from my shelf—
Alas, alack, I picked out
   The kind I like myself!

NOVEMBER 21, 1927

A Housewife's Thanksgiving

Thanks give I, that I bought that large, plump bird—
    My frugal nature craved the smaller one.
When Aunt Nell and her boys walked in, I knew
    A twelve-pound turkey never would have done.

Thanks, that the twins ate too much yesterday!
    Today, they'll take care how they over-eat,
And not disgrace me with their starved-pup ways,
    Stuffing small paunches with the rich and sweet.

Thanks, that I got clean curtains hung in time;
    And that I didn't burn the pumpkin pie;
That late last night the country cider came;
    The nuts are good this year; the squash is dry.

Thanks give I that the cousins and the aunts
    Will wash the dishes when the fete is done.
I can use all my kettles, pots and pans,
    Then sit down afterwards and not wash one!

NOVEMBER 24, 1926

Gifts for Children

When I can't buy expensive toys,
 No longer do I sigh;
When fifty-dollar Play-mobiles
 Must calmly be passed by.

Last Christmas when small Sue received
 A rare old music box,
In half an hour she dropped it for
 Some paper building-blocks!

Tom's bosom friend has "tipped me off."
 Tom wants "The Raids of Morgan,"
(A volume from the ten-cent store!)
 And please, a real mouth-organ!

I need not feel distressed to buy
 The twins no blooded hound.
They gravely feel they should adopt
 An orphan from the Pound!

DECEMBER 20, 1926

Santa's Last Call

I think this will be Santa Claus' last year.
    There's too much wisdom going 'round our house.
The twins are questioning the ways of deer,
    And Tom frowns, silent as a wise young mouse.

For the last time the Christmas tree will shine
    With mystic glory, lit by magic hands.
For the last time the gifts beneath the pine
    Will hold the strangeness of his Arctic lands.

The toys next year will have an earthly twang.
    The tree won't seem so tall, so marvelous.
The stockings filled by mortal hands will hang
    Not quite so bulging or so glamorous.

I want to make for Santa's last farewells
    A fairyland of toys and lights and play;
And then he'll shake his sleigh's small silver bells,
    Click to his reindeer—and just slip away.

DECEMBER 21, 1926

Christmas Plum Pudding

Christmas calls for evergreens
    And sprigs of mistletoe,
For icicles along the eaves,
    And softly falling snow.

Red candles on the chimney-ledge
    Above the fire must glow,
And candy canes and animals
    In all the socks must go.

Then top the dinner and the day
    With Christmas pudding, stout
With raisins, citron, nuts and spice
    And brandy poured about.

Alight with holly on its breast
    And 'round its ample girth,
Plum pudding makes a holiday
    Of any day on earth!

DECEMBER 22, 1926

Trimming the Tree

(Suggested by Mrs. J. H. R.)

The Christmas-candle flame burns red,
The children are asleep in bed.
    Aunts, uncles, cousins come to see
    The trimming of the Christmas tree.

Tinsel and swinging birds appear,
With colored balls from yesteryear,
    And violent arguments ensue
    In placing red and green and blue.

Then Uncle Ben hangs popcorn strings,
And candy canes, and saints with wings.
    And Aunt Mehitabel declares
    The stockings should be hung in pairs.

"The children's tree" is an excuse
For turning childish instincts loose;
    If adults didn't love to play,
    There'd be no trees on Christmas Day!

DECEMBER 23, 1926

Christmas Carols

Just for tonight the world will pause
    And give its common love a tongue,
In answer to the spirit's laws,
    When Christmas carols sweet are sung.

Candles in every house will glow;
    Just for tonight the streets will hum
With age-old music, soft and low,
    When Christmas carolers go and come.

There will be peace on earth, goodwill,
    And love for every living thing;
The bells will peal, the air will thrill,
    As silver-throated minstrels sing.

Ah, for so brief a little time
    The world with kindness is alight!
Out of the dark the carols' chime
    Just for tonight—just for tonight!

DECEMBER 24, 1926

A Glimpse of Santa

Four small pajama-ed forms crept down the stair,
　　Tom and the twins and small Sue in the rear,
Shivering in the dawn with hope and fear,
　　To see if Santa Claus had yet been there.

The street-lamps shone in on the Christmas tree
　　And touched the round glass balls with spots of light.
The four, as one, turned back again to flee,
　　Scrambling past one another in mad flight.

"Don't anyone go down!" Tom panted. "Santa's there!"
　　His heart was beating in his small slim throat.
"We saw him plainly, coming down the stair—
　　We saw the buttons shining on his coat!"

DECEMBER 14, 1927

The Week after Christmas

(With Apologies to the Old Classic)

'Twas the week after Christmas, and all through the
house
Were the signs of the annual Yuletide carouse.
    Gifts were unboxed with no pretense of care,
    Their wrappings in every available chair.

The Christmas tree candles were burned to the end.
The tree had grown wobbly and threatened to bend.
    The holly hung crooked at window and door,
    The tinsel and cotton were strewn on the floor.

The boxes of candy all week had grown thinner,
And no one was hungry for breakfast or dinner.
    I nibbled at fruits and at nuts on the shelf,
    And seemed to feel rather peculiar myself.

With rooms in a glorious, toy-filled confusion,
With cakes unforbidden and sweets in profusion,
    The week after Christmas puts gray in my hair—
    The children's delight and the housewife's despair!

DECEMBER 27, 1926

Relatives and Friends

Treasure

I shan't send Tom on errands for a while.
    My discipline shall be a trifle soft.
Not mine the words to bring him back to earth.
    He's reading "Treasure Island" in the loft.

He walks with Long John Silver, and the sea
    Beats with its music on his startled ears;
And old blind Pew will take him by the hand,
    And stick a-tap, will lead him down the years.

He treads the ground unseeing, starry-eyed;
    Plays, eats and sleeps and studies in a trance.
His mind consorts with pirates and with ships,
    In high adventure. He has found romance.

Not mine the voice to call him from the realm,
    Where sailors' parrots cry and silver gleams!
He has found treasure past life's power to steal.
    He's keeping company, these days, with dreams.

NOVEMBER 4, 1926

Aunt Ida's Letters

I'd know Aunt Ida's letters blind.
They're small and plump like her! And kind!
   Why, when I touch the envelope,
   I feel her love, her cheer, her hope.

The lines meander on the page.
"I guess it is a sign of age,"
   She writes, "to chat and ramble so."
   The dearest rambling that I know!

She tells me what she had for tea,
When friends dropped in. And I can see
   A picture of her smiling there,
   The lamplight silver on her hair.

And through her talk of life, and things,
The beauty of her spirit sings.
   And when her letter-writing's done,
   There will be somehow less of sun.

DECEMBER 4, 1926

The Family Album

(Suggested by Mrs. L. F. D.)

Look at Aunt Minnie's frizzled hair!
That parasol! That startled stare!
   And Grandpa on the other page,
   When bicycles were all the rage!

The pompadours, the folded hands!
Group-pictures of the Ladies' Bands!
   Mustaches like a crop of oats:
   Gold teeth and bangles; skin-tight coats!

Plump Floradora girls with fans,
And mammoth hats, and smirking glance;
   Aunt Em's twelve offspring, side by side;
   A bridegroom and his blushing bride!

May Heaven forgive my ribald mirth—
Each one must take his turn on earth.
   My heirs, in course of time, will be
   Convulsed at photographs of me!

FEBRUARY 9, 1927

The Railroad Station

Tomorrow, from the distant West,
　　Aunt Em arrives. Bill's due from Rome.
I look for Sue and all the rest—
　　My roving folks are coming home!

A year ago the enemy-train
　　Snorted along its outbound track.
A friend—forgotten, now, my pain—
　　It's bringing all the family back!

My sudden friendliness, no doubt,
　　For railroad stations, comes when calls
Report trains coming in—not out!
　　Today, I love those smoky walls!

The railroad station thrills my heart—
　　The folks will meet there, to a man—
For it unites, that one did part—
　　The outpost of our gathering clan!

AUGUST 23, 1927

Aunt Em's Antiques

"Are those 'antiques'?" Aunt Emmy sniffed
   In disapproval most emphatic.
"I wouldn't have them as a gift—
   I've hid their doubles in my attic.

"That vase you think's so grand and fine
   Was just a pickle-jar, I know.
That cooky-crock, like one of mine,
   Cost ten cents, ninety years ago.

"Such prices, for such worn old stuff!
   For antiques, give me a brass bed.
Hooked antique rugs? Not good enough!
   I'll take mine new!" Aunt Emmy said.

DECEMBER 9, 1927

Aunt Em on Patchwork Quilts

You praise patch-quilts, (old Aunt Em said)
Pieced o' folks' garments, for a bed.
They're good enough, as beddin' goes,
But what I say is, Who wore the clothes?

Now take your quilt you brag up so.
You see that green-striped calico?
That was an apron Sal Jenks wore—
The town's disgrace—in 'eighty-four.

Those red squares came from Ed Smith's wife.
Ed was the town's prime cause o' strife.
I'd do no sleeping, I declare,
Near that scamp's red flannel underwear!

FEBRUARY 24, 1928

The Horrors

I get the horrors when I think of this:
   The sight of "company" coming down our street—
It makes my heart-beats flutter, skip and miss—
   With simply nothing in the house to eat!

I get the horrors in the afternoon
   If female footsteps sound outside the door—
My breath inside feels like a burst balloon—
   And I'm just scrubbing up the kitchen floor.

The horrors seize me when I realize
   I've asked the Joneses to dine from out of town,
On just the night the folks they most despise,
   The Perkins, always plan on driving down.

But these are pleasures to my agony,
   When Aunt Janette swoops down, with silken swishes,
And I can't find, not for the life of me,
   Enough clean tea-towels for the dinner dishes!

JUNE 20, 1927

My Friend's Relations

(Suggested by Mrs. B. L. C.)

I've never met her kith and kin
    And yet I know them all;
On Pa's side they are dark of skin
    And all Ma's folks are tall.

I've never seen her maiden aunts—
    My land, those girls are neat.
But I should know them at a glance
    On any city street.

She is an artist, with a stroke
    Describing some odd trait.
I know how Uncle Eb awoke
    And how Aunt Emmy ate.

And when my friend comes visiting,
    I entertain a throng,
Old friends of mine. She seems to bring
    Her kith and kin along!

JANUARY 20, 1928

Killed with Kindness

I've been visiting
    Here and there,
And I'm almost done-up,
    I declare!

At Cousin Sue's
    We ate and ate,
And now I'm twelve pounds
    Over-weight.

At Cousin Sue's
    We "bridged" and "tea-ed,"
Lost hours of sleep,
    And I'm still weak-kneed.

I've been visiting
    East and West;
I'm killed with kindness
    And I'm home to rest!

SEPTEMBER 30, 1927

Uncle Abner

Great-Uncle Abner wanted, just once more,
    To dress as Santa Claus and trim the tree.
Altho' his hand shook and his beard was hoar,
    He made the finest Kriss you'd want to see.

He said he'd like to carve the Christmas goose
    Just once again; the slices paper-thin;
Then, swimming in its own rich fruity juice,
    Proudly to bear the burning pudding in.

May he in Heaven trim a mighty spruce
    With stars and planets, for the cherubim!
And may there be a great celestial goose,
    And pudding lit with meteors, for him!

DECEMBER 20, 1927

The Points of View

(Suggested by Mrs. G. D., Shortsville, N.Y.)

When Emma comes to visit,
    She cleans my house each day.
She has the strangest notions
    Of what is work and play.

For she despises cooking,
    The nicest work I know,
But loves to clean the cupboards,
    And shelves that never show!

I feel so conscience-stricken—
    When I visit her, I shirk.
I only do the cooking,
    While Emma does the work.

But I heard her tell a caller,
    "Ah, friends like mine are few.
She's doing all my work. She has
    The queerest point of view!"

AUGUST 18, 1926

The Fallen Idol

I've often served my dinner late—
  Most women have—when clubs detained me.
Shamed, while my hungry children wait,
  The thought of Emma Smith's sustained me.

At least there's one of us, I thought,
  A credit to her sex and calling,
Who always does things when she ought.
  With her, no tardiness, no "stalling."

Alas, tonight at half-past six
  I saw her rushing home, poor woman,
Plainly in a tardy fix.
  The best of us, it seems, is human!

FEBRUARY 22, 1928

Secrets

For pumpkin pie I'm noted.
  About this time of year
Pleas for its sacred secret
  With jealous looks, appear.

No one has guessed it must be mixed
  Just thin enough to "slosh,"
Or that instead of pumpkin, ah,
  I use a Hubbard squash!

The flavor of my pumpkin pie
  Is touted far and wide.
Why then reveal, betray my art,
  The secrets of my pride?

I'd like to serve with it, the cheese
  Em Seaton moulds in jell,
But how she makes that delicacy,
  The selfish thing won't tell!

NOVEMBER 18, 1926

The Need of Change

Miranda Perkins feeds her Jim
    The most delicious dishes.
She caters to his every whim
    And gastronomic wishes.

And all his life she's set him down
    To meals that kings might order:
Braised southern chicken, golden-brown,
    With sweetbreads for a border!

Well, in a restaurant last night
    Jim Perkins was bespoken—
Eating beans with all his might!
    Miranda's heart was broken.

The moral, as I told her then,
    Is nothing new or strange:
The best-fed, petted, pampered men
    Most feel the need of change!

FEBRUARY 22, 1927

Em Seaton's Cake Tree

It was the wonder of my childhood days—
    The way Em Seaton's cakes grew on a tree!
    There they all hung, as natural as could be,
Right on the twigs, before our youthful gaze.

Em kept a three-foot stripling tree, it seems,
    Just for this purpose—varnished, shiny, straight—
    To deck with cup-cakes. We could scarcely wait—
The cake tree gave us food for months of dreams.

Twice yearly for us were the stiff boughs spread
    With black cakes, white, and brown ones rich and spiced,
    Speckled with caraway or thickly iced,
Dotted with cinnamon drops of fiery red.

This was a miracle to us so strange,
    There must be forests with a magic name
    From whence Em Seaton's cake tree came—
Somewhere, we thought, beyond all grief, all change.

AUGUST 24, 1927

Caught

I've held my head most awfully high
At Annie Perkins going by.
She buys the baker's bun and scone,
While I, proud housewife, make my own.

But yesterday I was so late
That, not to make my family wait
For dinner while I made one, I
Stopped at the bake-shop for a pie.

No more 'twixt her and me a wall—
After my pride, behold my fall!
The ways of Providence do awe me—
For who but Annie Perkins saw me!

NOVEMBER 26, 1927

New Neighbors

The new house, building just across the way,
    Is finished, and the folks are moving in.
They're cleaning up the scraps of wood today.
    And the new grass is showing, pale and thin.

What kind of people are they? No one knows.
    They have three children, and their name is Brown.
They look respectable, and wear good clothes.
    They're here to stay, with business in the town.

Their furniture looked just about like ours
    When they unloaded. Decent, good—but worn.
It's a good sign to see those ferns and flowers.
    Her curtains are nice; one's mended where it's torn.

Just wait a minute—call it fair or foul,
    I have a method never yet proved wrong . . .
I went and waved at her with my dish towel—
    And, say, she waved right back! Yes, they "belong!"

APRIL 27, 1927

Neighbors' Cats

I hanker for my neighbor's cat.
    A feline prince, untamed and wild.
The cats I've owned have always been
    So stupid, tame and tabby-mild.

I've never had a cat so proud,
    So green-eyed, black and smooth as silk,
I've never had a cat who lapped
    So haughtily, his bowl of milk!

Why did Fate choose my neighbor's home
    Instead of mine, for such a king?
I covet him, from paws to purrs—
    I've even thought of kidnaping!

And yet my neighbor said today,
    "Oh, he's too wild—and such a size.
But say, that cat you used to have—
    That Persian with the amber eyes!"

AUGUST 21, 1926

Friends by Sight

I see each day a dozen folks
    Whom life across my pathway sends,
And though we speak no greeting words,
    We are companions, we are friends.

An old man on a knotted cane
    Limps by when afternoon grows late;
I nod, behind my window-pane;
    He bows, as he goes past my gate.

A farmer, who twice weekly goes
    To market, waves his whip at me.
A stout policeman tweaks his cap,
    And smiles in camaraderie.

They come from nowhere, and they go
    Unknown and nameless, day and night.
But life is sweeter for the nods,
    The passing, of my friends-by-sight.

NOVEMBER 15, 1926

Handsome Is as Handsome Does

Minerva Jenkins' form and face
    Are plain past help of art,
But you should see her breakfast rolls
    And taste her apple-tart!

Minerva Jenkins on the street
    Goes unobserved of men,
But when she turns a pudding out,
    You ought to see them then!

Her costumes are the town's despair,
    Her hats are weird and wan,
But she sets styles in cooking, when
    She puts an apron on!

If beauty trials were ever held
    Across a tray of pies,
With hungry men as judges there,
    Minerva'd take the prize!

JUNE 3, 1927

Sounds on Our Street

If you should happen down our street
    These Summer evenings, you would hear
    Neighbor-sounds from far and near,
And busy neighbor-feet.

You'd hear dishwashing, finished quick,
    You'd hear the playing children shout,
    With ice cream being ladled out,
And late lawn mowers' click.

You'd hear the Jenkins' Ford drive in,
    And Jones' old Airedale trotting home,
    You'd hear boys whistling on a comb,
And radios begin.

You'd hear folks chatting at their doors,
    And Sal, the gossip, make her rounds.
    These are the street's same evening sounds
You hear, I think, on yours!

JULY 14, 1927

The Home Town

The home-town is the only place
Where even strangers know your face,
   Through family likeness and declare,
   "That must be Jane's girl over there!"

And there the village gossip halts
To call to mind your childhood faults,
   The fearful things you did when small,
   Your sins with stone and bat and ball.

The dogs that pass you on the street,
The very children that you meet,
   All seem to recognize and know
   This was your home, too, long ago.

And in the old home-town there lives
The warmth that long acquaintance gives;
   And as the friendly teapot smokes,
   Old ladies nod, "I knew your folks!"

MAY 26, 1927

Sal Jenks' Window

A window is both ear and eye,
To hear and see the world go by;
    A peep-hole opening on the street,
    Where pass such entertaining feet!

Sal Jenks has sat by hers for years—
And what she sees, and what she hears,
    With ears well-cocked and straining look,
    Would make a village history book!

"Set long enough, and you can see
Most anything," she said to me.
    "And what I hear, as folks go by,
    Would open up a body's eye."

"That's why my window's kept so clean,"
She says, "so nothing'll go unseen."
    In March, she lets the wind blow through,
    For fear she'll miss a word or two!

MARCH 17, 1927

Crazy Nell

I called on crazy Nell today,
Who lives on down the Pike a way.
   They say she's mad as August's moon
   And has grown old and gray too soon.

The path that led me to her door
Was pebbled like the ocean's floor
   With shiny stones. Her crumbling cabin
   Was bordered 'round with ragged-robin.

Her stoop was buried under phlox,
Her windows hid by hollyhocks,
   And on Nell, rocking in the sun,
   Fell clematis petals, one by one.

A wild rose in her hair was caught,
Her hands were filled with flowers. I thought,
   Seeing this metamorphosis:
   "Can madness be where beauty is?"

SEPTEMBER 1, 1927

The Jesters

I heard a warbling in the street,
So high, so throbbing and so sweet,
    The king of all the birds must be,
    Thought I, a-making minstrelsy.

And then I saw him—Dan M'Groun,
In rags from shirt to breeks to shoon,
    And playing on a pipe so small
    It scarcely was a pipe at all.

Dan looked at me and grinned and took
His pipes from out his lips and shook
    With mirth that wrinkled his old hide
    Like cracking leather, weather-dyed.

I frowned and took myself away.
"I'll not be fooled again today,"
    I said that evening when I heard
    Someone a-chortling like a bird.

But there beside me on a tree
A robin cocked one eye at me.
    'Twas he had sung, and I was daft,
    The fat red rascal chirped—and laughed!

SEPTEMBER 3, 1927

The Miser

When Prudence Payne has company
    Her heart with misery fills;
They are not eating steaks, to her
    They're eating dollar bills.

She gave her cousin Mary Jane
    A crystal choker collar.
Alas, each bead to Prudence Payne
    Shone like a silver dollar.

She shudders when the furnace man
    The glowing fire has coaled.
He isn't shoveling coal, to her—
    He's shoveling lumps of gold!

JANUARY 17, 1928

Philosophical Nuggets

Work and the Weather

I like tasks better if they suit the day—
   Work to the weather should adapt itself.
When hours hang heavy and the sky is gray,
   I really like to clean a pantry shelf!

When winds are blowing through the shrubs and trees,
   Hurrying home the tardy lady-bugs,
And all the world seems flapping in the breeze,
   I like to join right in and shake my rugs!

I like to do my mending when the rain
   Hushes the world and quiets passing feet.
It's restful then, to darn a counterpane,
   To sit and think, and make my patching neat.

And when white clouds lie idle in the sky,
   The hot sun's drowsy and the fat bees shirk,
Passing the hard-to-enter posies by—
   It seems plain foolish to do any work!

MAY 25, 1927

The Day's Work

Another day is done,
  Finished and spent.
What has my long toil won?
  Only—content.

Twilight lies soft around,
  Day's noises cease.
Weary, what have I found?
  Only—deep peace.

What has the day's work brought?
  A child's caress,
A smile, a friend, a thought,
  Just—happiness.

I gave my hours, my self,
  My time's small hoard.
Love, that shy, wayward elf,
  Was my reward!

AUGUST 22, 1927

The Easiest Way

"I will not scrub that wall," I said,
    "Tho' years of dirt and dust imbue it.
My laziness be on my head—
    It's too hard work. I shall not do it."

But past it, back and forth each day,
    It was so shockingly unsightly
My mind and nerves almost gave way,
    And I grew sleepless, tossing nightly.

At last one morning I gave in,
    Took pail and brush and grumbled "Drat it!"
Hard work? I might as well begin—
    It's easier than looking at it!

DECEMBER 3, 1927

At Night

At night, folks sort of take their ease.
They let the cat drowse on their knees,
    They watch the grate-fire glowing bright,
    And sit and think and dream—at night.

The evening brings a calm content;
The work is done, the day is spent,
    And there's no need for thought or care—
    Just napping in an easy chair.

And no one talks or chatters much,
For friendly minds, when quiet, touch
    Without the need for speech; and find
    The silence grateful, sweet and kind.

And then Home lays its blessed bands
On children's faces, mother's hands,
    And draws them all together tight,
    Where Love sits by the hearts—at night.

JANUARY 8, 1927

The Fault

Is this one faulty? And does that one seem
Less lovely somehow, than the early dream?
    Are this friend's grave mistakes so plain to see,
    And does he disappoint and trouble me?

Am I annoyed by every small mistake
Those close to me, and well-beloved, make?
    Do I condemn the life they choose to live,
    And find it hard to pardon or forgive?

If all my thinking, all my thoughts, were kind,
If love filled up my spirit, heart and mind,
    The faults in them that chafe and anger me,
    I should not ever recognize or see.

Not mine the judgment on strange souls to pass,
Nor hold up to the world a looking glass.
    If I find men and women sorry stuff,
    The fault is mine—I have not loved enough.

MARCH 28, 1927

Voices I Love

Voices of those I love are sweet to hear,
  Of pleasing pattern and of soft design,
Because the words they say are for my ear,
  Messages spoken from their hearts to mine.

Voices of those I love make melody—
  Dear tunes, dear music, of the friendly word!
Sweeter and more beautiful to me
  Than Summer singing of the mocking-bird.

Voices of those I love are warm as sun,
  And stream, like sunshine, straight into my heart.
They may to others seem but drab and dun—
  Colored, to me, by love's consummate art.

Perhaps the soul speaks to the listening ear,
  And mind to mind and heart to heart are drawn;
For in my inmost self I still can hear
  Voices I love—long vanished and long gone.

MAY 11, 1927

Bread on the Waters

I gave a gift of posies
   From my small garden close,
And friendship came in quick return
   For every crimson rose.

I welcomed in a stranger,
   Giving my simple best,
And gratitude came swiftly
   For food and cheer and rest.

I gave love's crumbs, a handful,
   And love came back to me
In measure overflowing—
   A world of love, a sea!

JULY 15, 1927

The Heart on the Sleeve

"Don't wear your heart upon your sleeve,"
Wise men have said, but I believe
   The heart so worn, while liable
   To hurt, may be more pliable!

A heart exposed to every pain
Is one that holds no thought of gain;
   It loves, and gives unstintedly
   Affection and true sympathy.

A heart upon the sleeve is one
Laid bare to every bit of sun.
   It may be light or frivolous,
   But ah, it finds life marvelous!

It may be wise to shield the heart
And walk in safety quite apart,
   All hurt and sorrow far above.
   How stingy to be wise in love!

AUGUST 1, 1927

Envy

These things I envy richer folk
    As fierce as I am able:
House maids to water all the ferns
    And set the dinner table!

I feel no jealousy or greed
    Of trips in foreign air—
No quainter sights were ever seen
    Than at a county fair!

Their proud and glittering opera,
    Half-understood, half-heard,
Could never be so tuneful
    As a mating mocking bird.

I covet no display of wealth,
    Diamonds, pearls or sable,
But oh! someone to tend the ferns
    And set the dinner table!

JUNE 8, 1926

Jealousy

A nicer, greener lawn than mine
    Elicits my sincerest praise.
And I have never grudged my friends
    The flowers and vegetables they raise.

But there's a honeysuckle vine,
    And there's a climbing rambler rose,
Across my next door neighbor's porch,
    That cause me many jealous throes.

They grow together, intertwined,
    One fragrant rose and cream bouquet,
And make her simple little house
    A gorgeous, breath-taking display.

That vine-bouquet is my despair,
    And I am jealous through and through;
Because, if I'd been smart, I could
    Have planted mine together, too!

AUGUST 16, 1926

The Weak Spot

Most everyone has some weak spot
Where flattery, as like as not,
　　Can enter in, noon, night or day,
　　To steal the sense and wits away.

Now anyone can praise my clothes,
My hair, my figure or my nose,
　　And laughing up my two sleeves, I
　　Detect the trick behind the lie.

Folks can admire my spotless floors—
I know there's dust behind the doors;
　　I wonder, when they praise my mind,
　　What hidden axe they have to grind.

But when a stranger sits at table,
Eating as long as he is able,
　　And lauds my biscuits—why, my lands
　　I'm just like putty in his hands!

JANUARY 3, 1927

Samaritans Needed

I paused to match a spool of thread
    In the department store.
I could not tell which shade of red
    Matched that I'd had before.

And when I voiced my doubts, the crowd
    Of women closely pressed,
With one accord spoke up and vowed
    A certain shade seemed best.

I've had strange women touch my arm
    And give a warning pat
When I stood on the verge of harm
    In buying dress or hat.

Because a woman's shopping road
    So perilous is found,
We ban the usual female code—
    Samaritans abound!

MARCH 2, 1927

Blissful Ignorance

My wealthy hostess served her tea
    With linens choice, and silver;
But her fine china looked to me
    Peculiarly familiar.

"You like my plates, I see," she sighed.
    "You do so with good reason.
They're 'Royal Crown,' my greatest pride.
    I buy just one each season."

And then I placed the quaint design,
    The luster and the color—
Exactly like a plate of mine
    I'd found for half a dollar.

Almost the rarest china made!
    It dawned on me, poor sinner,
On "Royal Crown," quite undismayed,
    I'd been giving Puss her dinner!

AUGUST 6, 1927

When I Grow Old

Dear Mrs. Rawlings: When I am old, I want to live alone in a little
three-room cottage, surrounded by trees and flowers. What is your
idea of expressing this? Mary C. B.

I've had so much of houses and of "things,"
 So much of furniture, so much of stuff.
When I grow old, some cozy cubby-hole,
 A three-room cottage, will be big enough.

I've had so much of living in the world,
 Such busy days and people I have known.
I feel the need of wisdom and of peace—
 When I grow old, I'd like to be alone.

But I must have green grass and gayest flowers,
 With trees before my door, for rest and shade.
For I'll need Beauty when the time grows short.
 Surrounded thus, I shall not be afraid.

I want to pass the evening of my days
 Calmed by a sunny garden's tranquil hours.
After a hurried life, how sweet to stroll!
 To grow old gracefully, among the flowers!

SEPTEMBER 8, 1926

Old Clothes

I've turned my four-year-old "best dress"
So that the worn spot never shows.
I'll have to wear my suit again—
It should be pensioned, Heaven knows!

But I'll be in good company—
The nicest woman in our town
Has worn black silk for twenty years
And never seen a Paris gown!

And since my friends don't seem to mind
My costume's somewhat out of date,
I'll close my eyes to women's shops
And let the fashion writers prate!

For lovely clothes would not assure
A neighbor's warm and kindly smile.
Old friends forgive old clothes, because
Friendship is never out of style!

SEPTEMBER 16, 1926

A Field of Stubble

A field of stubble is a quiet thing.
  The Summer's over and the harvest done,
And there is only resting-still to do,
  And lying frosted under Autumn sun.

There has been fruitful toil and living there,
  Planting and growing, and then garnering,
The young grain reaped and sent across the world.
  A field of stubble is a lonely thing!

Harvest is always peaceful—always lone.
  The end of things is silvery and serene.
A field of stubble is a tale of life—
  Like scarred old quiet faces I have seen.

OCTOBER 14, 1926

The Hurdy-Gurdy

I danced to hurdy-gurdies
    In Spring, when I was young,
And rolled their foolish melodies
    Across my little tongue.

The world was gay and jolly,
    And so the tunes seemed sweet;
A young and laughing folly
    Was in my dancing feet.

The hurdy-gurdy playing
    Outside my housewife's gate
Sounds harsh—for hair is graying,
    And steps have grown sedate.

Not to the organ-grinder,
    I toss a silver dime,
But to the sweet reminder
    That I was young, one time.

APRIL 22, 1927

The Scientific Lecturer

(Suggested by Mrs. G. H. S., Rochester)

The scientific lecturer
Cried, "Never mind what you prefer,
    Just eat the things I say.
Don't touch the pastries that you crave,
You'll fill a plump and early grave,
    Or live to rue the day."

"Meat and potatoes never blend.
They mean a most untimely end.
    Don't ever eat hot bread."
He damned the very things I like.
There wasn't one he failed to strike.
    "Prolong your lives!"

I'll never go to hear, again,
Ascetic scientific men
    Of lean and hungry tongue.
For if I've got to live on figs,
On roots and herbs and parsley sprigs,
    I'd rather die while young!

FEBRUARY 2, 1928

Out of Things

I'm often "out of things." I can't be sure
    That unexpected guests will always find
A well-stocked pantry and an ice-box filled.
    My bake-day may be seven days behind!

I'm often out of sugar, eggs or flour,
    Essentials of a quick and tasty feast.
But no one need go really hungry home,
    And simple meals are healthier, at least!

I want to give my best, of course. But bread
    Will do as well as muffins, all agree.
Butter and milk may substitute for cream.
    I can serve coffee, if I can't serve tea!

But there's no substitute yet known for cheer.
    Food's for the moment, friendship, for all while.
And so I pray that I may never be
    Out of a welcome and a friendly smile.

JULY 6, 1926

Keeping Hold

How does a bird stay on the bough,
When wind and hail beat fiercely in,
When branches toss and scrape and lash,
Tumultuous in the tempest's din?

How does a butterfly still cling
To his frail, bending spear of grass,
Folding his airy, fragile wings
Until the beating rain shall pass?

How does a man or woman keep
Untarnished faith, and feel no fear,
When friends and life and love seem far,
And pain and death and sorrow, near?

Just as all creatures lift their heads,
In time of stress and trouble, bold,
They know all storms must surely pass—
And so they wait—and just keep hold!

SEPTEMBER 11, 1926

One Sunny Window

One sunny window
   Is enough for me;
One glimpse of sky
   Past a bending tree.

One warm window-ledge
   Where the kitten's curled.
One corner mine,
   Out of all the world.

One hour each day,
   To bask in sun,
In the afternoon,
   When my work is done.

I could be happy
   Unloved, alone,
With one sunny window
   All my own!

OCTOBER 22, 1926

There Are No Lonely Hours

There are no lonely hours when, somewhere, dwells
 Someone who'd spend them with you. Miles of space
Vanish as though you lived next-door again,
 When someone, somewhere, longs to see your face.

Old friends, old neighbors, gone to other towns,
 Are in my mind when hours are long and dull.
And when they too hold thought and love of me,
 The vacant time is lovely and is full.

There is no solitude when hearts commune.
 No house is empty and no house is sad,
No table solitary, and no hearth,
 When being there would make some other glad.

When in her garden some far-distant friend
 Remembers that she picks my favorite flowers;
When someone, somewhere, thinks of me and smiles,
 So long, for me, there are no lonely hours.

NOVEMBER 17, 1926

Two Pictures

I saw across a field today
  Wild strawberries aglow,
But memory pictured there instead
  A day of long ago.

I saw a curly-headed child,
  Sun-bonneted in blue,
And through the basket on her arm
  Wild strawberries peeped through.

I saw a dear form welcome her,
  And then that mother made,
With sunshine on the table there,
  Wild berry marmalade.

Two pictures lie in every scene—
  The real one that we see,
And like a half-remembered dream,
  The sweeter—Memory.

JUNE 27, 1927

Sounds in Silence

When all the house is quiet,
In the hush of afternoon,
I can hear the grate-fire crackle,
And the fat tea-kettle croon.

I can hear the old clock ticking
With its creaky, wheezy whirr,
And in the sunny kitchen
I can hear the kitten purr.

I can hear a field-mouse creeping
In the rafters overhead,
And the ruffled flounces stirring
On the tall four-poster bed.

I can hear a sparrow hopping
On the crumb-spread window-sill—
All the little sounds of silence,
When the house and hands are still.

JANUARY 29, 1927

One Step More

If I can take just one step more,
   I can go on.
Daylight will come—it came before,
   A lovely dawn.

If through one window I can stare,
   Then I can see
The world, as always, passing there—
   A part of me.

If just one thing in life seems sweet—
   A child, a flower—
I need not be afraid to meet
   Tomorrow's hour.

Life's pageant I shall not forsake.
   Hope holds the door
Wide open, if I still can take
   Just one step more.

JUNE 22, 1927

Some Day

Some day, when I am well-to-do,
I'll dress in sheer silk through and through,
    And I'll discard all underwear
    That shows the smallest hole or tear.

Some day, if I am ever able,
I'll have flowers always on the table.
    My handsome silverware will shine—
    But not through any toil of mine!

I'll use the best, most fragile glasses,
Some day, when in the affluent classes.
    When in the dishpan then they shatter,
    I'll just buy more, and it won't matter.

This day, of which all housewives dream,
Has linen sheets, and floors a-gleam,
    And some day—this I strongly feel—
    I'll have fresh napkins every meal!

JUNE 23, 1927

The Beauty Parlor

My face is not my fortune,
   And so it seems to me
A little beautifying
   Not quite amiss might be.

I had a tonic treatment,
   A shampoo, a marcel;
I had a "pack," a "facial,"
   And eye-brows "plucked" as well.

They "touched me up" and rouged me,
   Put henna on my hair;
I was completely ruined
   When I went out of there!

Since from the beauty parlor
   I only turn out worse,
Hereafter, this my motto:
   Let Nature take her course!

MAY 14, 1927

Candlelight

(Suggested by M. S. L., Rochester, N.Y.)

Four tall slim candles cast their light
Across the glass and silver here;
Upon the napery white and sheer
Their waving shadows rest tonight.

Here peace and loveliness abide;
Beneath their flame a feast is spread
On sparkling plates of golden bread,
And every dish is glorified.

The commonplace has slipped away;
Here where a tapering candle gleams
We are the kings and queens of dreams,
For Beauty lights the every-day.

NOVEMBER 8, 1927

Stolen Fruit

I passed a farmer's orchard
 And was suddenly possessed
By memories of my childhood days
 When stolen fruits seemed best.

I slipped across the wooden fence
 And stole a peach or two,
But all the time my conscience cried,
 "Why, this is wrong to do!"

The stolen fruit seemed tasteless,
 My fingers turned to ice.
So I hunted up the farmer
 And I paid top-market price!

OCTOBER 11, 1927

My Conscience

My conscience will not let me shirk
 While other folks are busy.
I am compelled to rise and work
 Altho' my head grows dizzy.

I cannot take an easy chair
 And delve into my reading;
With another woman toiling there,
 I cannot sit, unheeding.

I've often forced my friends to leave
 Their work, at my insistence,
And in this way I can relieve
 The strain upon my conscience!

NOVEMBER 4, 1927

Duty Books

I don't like books I "ought to read."
    Too dull and ponderous, stupid stuff
I give scant interest and scant heed—
    Less weighty tomes have charm enough.

I do not care to read by rule,
    To follow where the critics swarm.
I like, regardless of their "school,"
    The books that keep my spirit warm.

I like to browse in libraries
    And choose at random from a shelf;
To read and study as I please.
    My duty is to suit myself.

DECEMBER 19, 1927

Warming Up the Engine

I have an author-friend who'll write
In a cold barn-like room, at night.
Her mind is clear, her work is good—
All hail to her real hardihood!

That wouldn't suit me. I know better
Than to attempt the briefest letter
Under a frigid temperature.
It wouldn't half make sense, I'm sure.

My thinking-outfit works just right
Before a hearth-fire, hot and bright.
It warms the engine up, I've found,
And makes my mental wheels go 'round.

JANUARY 11, 1928

The Early Christmas Shopper

(Suggested by Mrs. A. T. R.)

She boasts of her preparedness—
   No human tongue can stop her.
Her Christmas gifts are boxed and tied—
   I loathe the early shopper!

She knits wool mufflers in July;
   At linen sales she lingers,
And in November, there she sits
   With smug and idle fingers!

Her wrapping paper's bought by Fall—
   Hear its obnoxious rustle!
Her smile is unendurable,
   When other women hustle!

But as in shopping mobs I spend
   My silver and my copper,
I'd give ten years of life to be
   An early Christmas shopper!

OCTOBER 21, 1926

Ballade of Accomplished Work

How it occurred, I do not know,
    I cannot guess, I dare not say,
Although I seemed unduly slow,
    I finished all my work today!

I planned to wash—I finished that
    Before the skies turned threatening gray.
I trimmed a long-neglected hat.
    I finished all my work today!

Never before have plans come out
    In this complete, delightful way.
Incredible! Yet there's no doubt
    I finished all my work today!

    L'Envoi
Tell me the secret of my feat!
    How did I manage it, I pray?
These sweet words daily I'd repeat:
    I finished all my work today!

APRIL 19, 1927

Fooling Around

Some days I only fool around.
Perhaps I weed a patch of ground,
   Or trim one corner of the lawn—
   And then I give it up, and yawn.

Perhaps I pick the polish up
And shine one single silver cup—
   And then I leave the mess right there,
   To dust a bit, or wash my hair.

Perhaps I start some home-made bread—
Then order baker's rolls instead.
   I wash a towel, or iron a bit,
   A shirt or two—and then I quit.

You ask, why do I work at all
With my accomplishment so small.
   Well—fooling around's not strenuous,
   And yet I still feel virtuous!

JUNE 2, 1927

A Guilty Conscience

I idled yesterday away—
So I am filled with zeal today,
    Intent on making recompense
    For past housekeeping negligence.

I took a walk, I had a nap,
I held the kitten in my lap;
    I meant to dust, but read instead.
    At 8, last night, I went to bed.

Today, I've dusted, swept and scrubbed,
And polished silver—how I rubbed!
    I've made some cookies, pie and cake;
    Cut out a dress I hope to make.

I do not owe my vim to rest,
Nor to my natural working zest.
    Although I'm still inclined to shirk,
    A guilty conscience makes me work!

JUNE 21, 1927

Too Much Energy

I started out my day at dawn
    Brimful of vim and life.
I planned to dig around the lawn
    Where weeds were growing rife.

I planned great tasks for all the hours—
    I meant to work all day.
But first, I thought, I'll pick some flowers
    To make a fresh bouquet.

I had such wealth of time to spare,
    Such energy and strength.
I bustled here and puttered there,
    And did small jobs at length.

I fussed at trifles merrily,
    And found at set of sun
I'd used up all my energy—
    But left my work undone!

SEPTEMBER 19, 1927

A Cure for Work

Too much of work, we all agree,
Is bad for folks like you and me.
It frays the housewife's tangled nerves
And spoils the very food it serves!

Too much to do day after day,
All work and worry, without play,
Make up a serious housewife's ill
Past help of tonic, herb or pill.

What can a weary woman do
With tasks that must be gotten through?
With work around, above, below?
The cure is simple: let it go!

The house will turn into a sight?
Well, let it turn, then—that's all right.
The Heavens will crash, in storm and squall?
Why, that's the treatment! Let them fall!

SEPTEMBER 21, 1927

Fooling Myself

With some unpleasant task to do,
   That's almost certain-sure to bore me,
Like lightning from the sunny blue
   I find some other work before me!

Confronted by a pile of socks
   In desperate need of careful mending,
I feel impelled to weed the phlox
   That went all Summer without tending.

While letters, long-unanswered, wait—
   A chore I have for days been dreading—
I am possessed, as sure as fate,
   To air the mattresses and bedding!

I fool myself elaborately,
   Some other line of work pursuing.
I seize each task so eagerly—
   Except the one I should be doing!

SEPTEMBER 27, 1927

Some Other Time

I have a trick—and no doubt you
Are guilty of it sometimes, too—
Of leaving stupid work undone
Until some more propitious sun.

"I'll feel like doing it tomorrow,"
I tell myself. And to my sorrow
Days, weeks and months have sometimes passed
Before I've done the job at last.

I must control my whims, my fancy—
It makes accomplishment too chancy.
To put unpleasant work away
Merely postpones the evil day!

JANUARY 14, 1928

Temptation

(Suggested by Emma D. C.)

Of course the house-tops wouldn't fall
If I didn't dust at all;
    If I let the sweeping go,
    And didn't mend or darn or sew.

Nothing grave would overtake
The household, if I didn't bake;
    If I calmly sat and read,
    And didn't make a single bed.

No one would decline and die
If I never made a pie;
    Or if I laid the wash away
    To fold and iron some other day.

This is temptation's subtle plea,
To make a lazy wretch of me;
    To egg me on to loaf and shirk,
    On days I just don't feel like work!

MARCH 16, 1927

Hospitality

I was a stranger and you took me in.
   You shared your table and fine fare with me;
Your choicest linens and your china thin
   Were placed before me when we sat at tea.

Your hands were generous. You gave your best,
   Choice dishes and rare fruits before me spread.
Soft pillows soothed me for my nightly rest,
   And downy covers lay upon my bed.

But did you know these things material
   Welcomed me less than those that have no form?
It was your kindness that was beautiful,
   It was your spirit's grace that kept me warm.

You called me friend. You made me one of you.
   I was no more a stranger and apart.
You give to hospitality a clue—
   Finer than open hands, the open heart.

JULY 28, 1927

Nature and the Natural

Earth's Children

These are Earth's children: leaves and fruits and flowers,
　　Nursed by the rain and sun's good nurturing;
Earth blossoms fair in those maternal hours,
　　Proud of her children, when men say "It's Spring!"

Apples have fallen ripely to the ground;
　　The ruddy, weary maple leaves lie deep;
The snow's warm blanketings will wrap them 'round;
　　Earth's red-cheeked children have come home to sleep.

To sleep—to plant their seeds, enrich her soil,
　　New beauty to the next new year to give;
Earth is repaid for all her love and toil—
　　Her immortal children have come home—to live!

NOVEMBER 29, 1927

A Rendezvous

Good-bye, petunias! And do you sleep
   Snug in your seeds, as any bug!
Sweet roses, pansies do you cuddle deep
   Under the snow's white velvet rug.

I'll spend the chill months at my household tasks,
   Keeping my family warm and fed.
While, where my garden in the pale sun basks,
   You'll drowse the Winter through—in bed!

Our paths must separate these many moons,
   You'll go your way while I go mine.
But when the wind of Winter o'er you croons,
   Ah, will you long for warm sunshine?

Sleep, then, and dream of being beautiful!
   Or dream of almost anything—
But don't forget, when April's at the full,
   That we've a rendezvous with Spring!

OCTOBER 11, 1926

The Look of Spring

There is no sunshine in the air,
　No birds come back to sing,
But still the tall old willows wear
　The lovely look of Spring.

Something of green life, young and free,
　Upon their branches lies.
Their ancient heads lift gracefully
　Against the Winter skies.

And I have known old folks, whose years
　Are only Time's white snows,
Through which the look of Spring appears
　And on their faces glows.

The spirit knows no age, no time.
　Its boundless youth can bring,
Across the hills of life we climb,
　The young, fresh look of Spring.

FEBRUARY 24, 1927

Spring in the Larder

Spring is in the offing;
   I hear the hucksters call
Fresh southern strawberries,
   With prices not bad at all.

Rhubarb stalks and spinach
   From down New Jersey way,
Are in. The shad are running—
   I had shad roe today.

The butcher's selling bratwurst—
   Unfailing Spring-time cue!
Fresh eggs are cheap. Tomatoes
   Show a healthy hue.

The country butter's sweeter,
   With sun in every ounce.
Spring is in the larder—
   And that's the Spring that counts!

MARCH 19, 1927

Reminders

The wrens and robins nesting,
   The cries of fledglings faint,
Remind me that our cottage
   Must have a coat of paint.

New puppies and new kittens,
   And fluffy chicks, new-hatched,
Remind me that my youngsters
   Must have some clothing patched.

The apple trees are budding,
   The crocuses appear—
And all these things remind me
   I need new shades this year.

You'll gather the connection
   If, like me, you've been blind
To things that needed doing,
   'Til Spring slipped up behind!

MARCH 31, 1927

A Boy, a Dog, an April Day

A boy, a dog, an April day—
    Bring these together, and you find
A perfect consonance of play,
    Three mischiefs with a single mind!

Along the fresh green budding lanes
    The trio loves to romp and race,
And blowing with the weather-vanes,
    To ferret out Spring's hiding place.

Nosing across each fragrant hill,
    Jumping each crevice, hole and brook,
They follow only wind and will,
    And find the world a picture-book.

Free and untrammeled, young and gay,
    Life lays kind hands on them to bless;
A boy, a dog, an April day—
    A trinity of happiness!

APRIL 2, 1927

Spring Is a Housewife

Spring is a housewife, full of vim
    To clean the musty world.
Winter? She has no use for him,
    About his hearth-fire curled!

She tweaks him by his reddened nose
    And sings her battle-song.
She makes him pack his tattered clothes
    And move his bones along.

She blows out smoke he left behind,
    His ashes, grime and soot.
She has Spring cleaning on her mind,
    And housework is afoot.

Then when his tracks are cleared away
    She brings out song and sun,
Decks out the world with posies gay—
    Her housewife's job is done!

MAY 9, 1927

Easter Clothes

All the wide world, more or less,
Will come out in new Easter dress,
    In fabrics gay, in colors high,
    And styles pretentious. Why not I!

The gnarled trees are dressed up once more.
The maple by my kitchen door
    Is flaming-red. The beech leaves shine.
    Must I do less in dress of mine?

In costumes fashionable will come
The whole of female Christendom.
    New hats, bags, dresses, shoes, will bring
    Tribute to Easter and to Spring.

With man and nature dressing bright
It seems but fair, but just, but right,
    To help dispel the Winter's gloom
    By also bursting into bloom!

APRIL 15, 1927

Easter Lilies

Sweet, sweet as bells in Paradise
   The Easter chimes are ringing;
Upon the air of morning rise
   Young dewy voices, singing.

More beautiful before the Lord
   Than hymn or harp or psalter,
Spring, for His rising-up, has poured
   White lilies on His altar.

Birth out of dying—this they prove;
   Earth joyous after sorrow;
Beauty they promise man, and love,
   Tomorrow and tomorrow.

His symbol in their hearts of gold—
   God, Beauty, Man, in union.
They are white hands cupped to hold
   The sweet wine of communion.

APRIL 16, 1927

June Is So Sweet

June is so sweet with posy-smells,
With pinks and Canterbury bells,
    With spicy rhododendron whiff,
    That all the month I sniff and sniff.

June is so sweet with robins' song,
With blue-birds trilling all day long,
    With wrens a-chirp from morn 'til night,
    I listen in with all my might.

June with its sun-kissed fruit is sweet,
With such delicious things to eat,
    That I spend hours with recipes,
    To dress each dish to tempt and please.

I might regret to see June go,
But strawberries are due, I know,
    And when I think of cherry pie—
    Why, I can't wait for sweet July!

JUNE 13, 1927

The Breath of Summer

White ruffled curtains stirring
    Across my window-sill
Move with the sun-warmed breezes
    From some bright distant hill.

All through my house is fragrance
    From garden and from lawn;
The scent of pinks and roses
    Stole through the air at dawn.

The golden sunlight flickers
    Across my shining floor;
The honeysuckle's nodding
    Beside the kitchen door.

The wings of Beauty flutter
    And are not far away.
The warm, sweet breath of Summer
    Blows through my house today.

JUNE 29, 1927

A Cricket in the House

I know that Summer's ended
    Its sunny, gay carouse,
When, chirping at my feet, I find
    A cricket in the house!

His busy pipe reminds me:
    Have I canned fruit enough?
It's not too late to make more jam,
    Or put up plums for duff!

Are coal and firewood ordered?
    Are stoves in good repair?
And have I any stock on hand
    Of Winter underwear?

It takes his shrill announcement
    My sense of time to rouse.
I'd be behind all Fall, without
    A cricket in the house!

SEPTEMBER 15, 1926

Apples Dropping

I watched the blossoms in the Spring,
   I saw the young green fruit grow round,
And now, as winds blow loud, I hear
   The apples dropping on the ground.

The grass is red with ripened fruit,
   And from my window I can see
The children gathering it there,
   Under the broad, frost-yellowed tree.

All day they loosen and they fall,
   To rest in earth's brown, leafy bed,
And on the roof at night I hear
   The apples dropping overhead.

Apples dropping in the Fall,
   Ending Spring and Summer times,
Mark musically the season's hour,
   And ring in Autumn with their chimes.

OCTOBER 20, 1926

October, Friend of Housewives

The Summer's play is jolly,
    And Summer guests are treats,
But I sometimes see their visits
    In terms of meals and sheets!

No company's so welcome
    But that it must be fed.
The well-loved guest from far away
    Must have a fresh-made bed.

Now the visitors have vanished,
    My Summer canning's done,
The children are packed off to school,
    Fall cleaning's not begun.

After a season's rushing,
    A Summer lived pell-mell,
October, friend of housewives,
    Has brought a breathing-spell!

OCTOBER 1, 1926

Plant Orphans

I've saved plant orphans, left to die.
   I prowled in every garden bed,
And rescued plump and lively ferns,
   Geraniums most fat and red.

I dug up some begonias,
   A fuchsia with its purple bell,
A maidenhair, a Wandering Jew,
   Some parsley, with its fresh green smell.

I potted them and brought them in,
   And set them on a sunny shelf,
Warm, safe and cozy in the house,
   Where I can bring them up myself.

And if the foundlings do not thrive,
   Nor like my care by any chance,
I'll turn them out again, and blame
   The base ingratitude of plants!

OCTOBER 29, 1926

Autumn's Carpet

Tread lightly on this lovely field,
For Fall has laid a carpet down
For Winter's silver shoe and gown,
Her crystal daintiness to shield.

Upon these asters, purple, white,
The frost and hail and ice will sift;
The snow will beautifully drift
Across this carpet of delight.

So red these sumac leaves, so fair,
So glorious the goldenrod,
It is a rug where even God
Might step, and pause, and wonder there.

OCTOBER 14, 1927

The Master Artist

There are no ugly gardens;
The colors all combine
With taste and grace more certain
Than artistry of mine.

Flowers always "go together."
No combination's "wrong";
For each bouquet is perfect,
Harmonious as a song.

There is no garish clashing
Of yellows, pinks, and blues,
Because a Master Artist
Blended and planned the hues.

NOVEMBER 16, 1927

The Maple Tree

When I am worn and wearied-out
And hours of work still walk about,
    I take my tiredness to the grass,
    Where bees and birds and beetles pass.

And then the kindly maple tree
Rustles her branches over me,
    Crooning a leafy lullaby
    All full of wind and clouds and sky.

Her brown roots are a cradle wide,
Where, snuggling by her quiet side
    I lose the years, the cares, the pain,
    And am a happy child again.

There's comfort in all rooted things,
The flower that sways, the pine that sings,
    And strength and joy return to me,
    Under the kindly maple tree.

JUNE 4, 1926

June Strawberries

June brings again my lilacs,
  Great bunches in my arms—
But June flowers, to my family,
  Have secondary charms.

I chat, unheard, of blossoms,
  Of nesting birds, of bees.
Before their annual hunger
  My June romancing flees!

For as the weeks go by us,
  The children are in fear.
"Oh, will there be, or won't there,
  June strawberries this year?"

How can I be romantic,
  And of June moonlight dream,
With all my household yearning
  For strawberries and cream!

JUNE 21, 1926

The Surprise Garden

Dear Mrs. Rawlings: Have you ever had the experience of planting certain seeds—and having something entirely different spring up? I call mine the surprise garden. Mrs. Katherine H.

I planted phlox and marigold,
 A poppy and a giant pink.
I had sweet William, columbine,
 And one verbena plant, I think.

The rains were soft, the sun was bright,
 The nights exactly warm enough.
I thought, "What posies I shall have—
 My garden's not had one rebuff."

Instead of pinks, nasturtiums grew!
 Calendulas, in place of phlox!
And where I'd planted columbine,
 There sprouted double hollyhocks!

I find I'm spoiled for gardens tame,
 With plants that grow by rule of thumb.
I much prefer to be surprised.
 I like my flowers adventuresome!

JULY 28, 1926

Dewberries

Be sure to wear a sunbonnet,
   For they grow only in the sun,
Across the clover-scented fields
   Their green and graceful tendrils run.

A two-quart granite pail will hold
   All you can pick in half a day.
They sweeten up on dewy nights,
   That's why they're "dew-berries," they say.

To put them in a berry pie
   Is desecration, nothing less.
Until you've eaten them with cream,
   You've tasted nothing, you'll confess.

Small cousins of the blackberry,
   In poor and sandy soil they live.
And like some folks, they're sweeter than
   The rich and haughty relative!

JULY 29, 1926

Shelling Peas

A gingham apron, wide and full,
　　A bushel basket full of peas,
A quiet, sunny afternoon
　　A hungry family to please!

By choice, a chair beneath a tree,
　　Altho' a shady porch will do.
A cooling breeze to brush my hands;
　　A bright new pan, by preference, blue!

I think of how, long years ago,
　　Grandmother shelled for seventeen!
I think of what a lovely gown
　　I'd like, of just that soft pea-green.

I think of how much toothsomeness
　　In one green, tight-sealed pod is held.
So, pondering on such pleasant things,
　　I find my bushel basket's shelled!

AUGUST 2, 1926

The Mint Bed

(Suggested by Mrs. Edgar T.)

I found a moist and shady spot,
    Among my ferns, where mint would grow.
I hid the budding sprigs with care—
    I wanted no one else to know.

I only gathered it at dusk,
    Away from sunlight's tell-tale glint.
But after all my well-planned care,
    The neighbors found my bed of mint!

They raided it with pleased surprise,
    They "borrowed" it for peas and lamb.
My mint provided half the town
    With flavor for its jell and jam!

Next year I'll plant the odorous sprays
    Beside the road, for all to see;
I can't combat the ancient law:
    Mint beds are public property!

AUGUST 4, 1926

Perennials

Sweet peas enchant me in July;
  Calendulas are my delight.
In Summertime nasturtiums flaunt
  Their gayety in colors bright.

Snapdragons are fair-weather flowers,
  Blooming if everything goes well,
And mignonette may condescend,
  If nursed, to cast its fairy spell.

But when these fragile blooms have passed,
  My staunch perennials endure;
Through snow and ice and winter gales,
  Phlox, marigold and pinks stand sure.

They're like the friendships that persist
  Through troubles, storms and sunless hours.
I love them for their loyalty—
  Perennial friends—perennial flowers.

AUGUST 6, 1926

Trees

Trees are like people, tall and thin,
   Short and round, and grave and gay,
They grow and bud and live and age,
   And move, in such a human way!

Poplars are very nervous folk,
   Forever wringing leafy hands.
A gnarled oak, battered down by time,
   Like some old battle chieftain stands.

An elm looks down with dignity
   Where red-cheeked apples bob and whirl,
Like jolly farm maids at a fair.
   A birch tree is a dancing girl.

Dear to my heart, the maple tree
   Above my gables nods and bends;
And plump and matronly it seems
   The kindliest of sheltering friends.

AUGUST 10, 1926

A Rainy Day

(Suggested by Mrs. Maud M. C.)

Sunshine means work-time; and on brisk, clear days
   I move in pace with all the bustling world.
My days pass busily, like rushing clouds,
   When winds blow crisply, and the leaves are whirled.

But when the soothing hush of rain comes down,
   And stills the wind and calms the poplar tree,
I find a peace, as though a door swung wide,
   With quiet rain the magic master-key.

A rainy day surrounds my busy house
   With coziness and calm, and hustle gone.
I hear the soft drops on the window-pane,
   And on my flowers, and on my freshened lawn.

Then with a book, and well-loved book-friends near,
   I sit and read and drowse and am content;
Forgetting cares and ills of work-a-day,
   Taking the lazy peace the rain has sent.

AUGUST 13, 1926

Wheat Fields

When I see wheat fields gleaming in the sun,
  Green in the Spring and golden in July,
I do not think of wheat kings' battles won
  But hungry little children trooping by.

I have no thought of speeding cars of grain,
  Of loaded wheat ships steaming into port—
I think of children standing in the rain,
  Waiting for rations of the bread-line sort.

I cannot think of wheat fields as a game,
  With brokers gambling on them in the marts.
With world-wide cries for bread, whose is the blame
  For hungry bodies and for hungry hearts?

Wheat fields were never meant to sell for gold!
  See, the wind ripples through them from the south,
And all the stalks like praying fingers fold,
  Longing to reach some famished little mouth.

SEPTEMBER 2, 1926

Petunia-Vain

(Suggested by Mrs. B—, Summerville, N.Y.)

I had some pink petunias
  In a sunny window-box,
The gayest posies on the street,
  In frilled and fluted frocks.

And since the folks who passed my house
  Admired their color so,
I placed a lamp nearby at night,
  The gorgeous tint to show.

I thought my vanity had passed
  Unnoticed, unobserved.
But, ah, my haughty spirit took
  The fall that it deserved!

For now, when I show pride in things,
  My friends remark, "It's plain,
She's all puffed up again! You know,
  She's pink-petunia-vain."

SEPTEMBER 4, 1926

Color-Mad

Something blue in every room;
  Somewhere, a touch of red;
A bit of purple on a couch,
  Or a pillow for my bed.

I had mauve draperies before—
  My new ones shall be green.
I must have yellow on a chair,
  Or on the fireside screen.

I'd love an orange breakfast nook,
  Or a violet dining-room,
Or any color ever mixed
  On any weaver's loom.

Not color-blind, but color-mad!
  I cannot get my fill.
When I was young, I fell in love
  With a rainbow on a hill!

SEPTEMBER 22, 1926

Apples

Apple cobbler, apple-cake,
    Apple sauce and apple pie—
No one can resist their taste,
    Or pass an apple dumpling by!

Cinnamon and powdered clove,
    Grated nutmeg, sugar, crumbs,
Make apple Betty fit for kings,
    And sweet as sugar-plums!

Apples by the bushel box—
    Everyone can help himself.
Children never beg for sweets,
    With apples handy on the shelf.

When Eve put her white hand forth
    And picked an apple from a tree,
She helped all housewives' menus out,
    And planned six months' desserts for me!

SEPTEMBER 24, 1926

A Geranium on the Shelf

They paint the modern kitchens
  With a fresco or a frieze—
But I'll have for decoration,
  A geranium, if you please.

It must stand above my table,
  On the shelf, beside the clock,
Where I see it while I'm cooking,
  While I sit and sew and rock.

Its gay red blossom matches
  My rag rug on the floor.
My kitchen glows a welcome
  When I step inside the door.

I shall hire no decorator,
  For I know a trick myself,
To make a kitchen cheery:
  A geranium on the shelf!

DECEMBER 15, 1926

Trees in Winter

Like friends who frown and turn away,
My jolly maples on the lawn
Grew chilly, bleak and harsh and gray.
My birch, my pear, seemed somehow gone.

Trees should be always gay and young,
I thought: not worn-out, tired and cold.
They should be fresh, with foliage hung.
They have no business looking old!

And then one day the snow came down
And gave the birch a samite cloak,
The maples each a silver crown;
Laid ermine on the royal oak.

Lovely as blossoming boughs in Spring,
Their branches shone. A blackbird came,
Delighted, and began to sing—
December had put June to shame!

JANUARY 11, 1927

Wind Tantrums

The wind beats on my window-pane,
He whirls my copper weather-vane,
  He whips the shrubs and lashes trees,
  Till everything before him flees.

He blows the snow from off my roof,
Snorts down the chimney in reproof.
  That I, who love a game of vim,
  Will not come out and play with him.

He rips my wet clothes off the line,
Undoing all that work of mine.
  He shakes the house and rattles doors,
  Then feeling huffier still, he roars!

To hear him rave, to see him frown,
You'd think the walls were coming down.
  Like any male by tantrums hit,
  He doesn't mean a word of it!

JANUARY 19, 1927

Hyacinths for the Soul

I went a-marketing today,
  My pantry shelves to fill,
But I came home, I grieve to say,
  With pots of daffodil.

I meant to spend my pennies there
  For vegetables and meat—
But, oh, the flower shops were so fair
  And smelled so fresh and sweet!

I stood and weighed a posy's charms
  Against a lettuce head;
And then I filled my hungry arms
  With hyacinths instead.

My house is full of perfumed bloom,
  But, ah, I feel a sinner!
My family, in deepest gloom,
  Ate bread and milk for dinner!

MAY 18, 1927

Lilac Time

I've laid aside my duster,
   I've put away my broom,
For just outside the window
   The lilacs are in bloom.

A misty rain is on them,
   And in the fragrant air
The purple clusters glisten—
   And I can only stare.

And I can only listen
   To those sweet notes I heard,
For in the bloom is hidden
   A plaintive phoebe-bird.

For I can sweep tomorrow—
   But in a silver rain
Phoebe-birds and lilacs
   May never meet again.

JUNE 4, 1927

The Face on the Pansy

There was an old man, long ago,
Who hated flowers and gardens so,
　That every one he came upon,
　The cranky rascal trampled on.

Now pansies were his special bane.
Their blossoms in those days were plain.
　Their simple blooms of black or yellow
　Seemed to enrage the poor old fellow.

He tore up pansies by the dozens,
And violets, their second-cousins,
　Until, if I am not mistaken,
　He was by palsy overtaken.

The pansies saw their chance to shock him,
In mischievous revenge to mock him;
　And to this day, to his disgrace,
　They wear his cross old bearded face!

JUNE 7, 1927

Sweet William

A gardener's daughter, long, long since,
In secret loved a handsome prince,
  Prince William, Scotland's boast and pride,
  The darling of the countryside.

Her father watched them meet one day
And saw Prince William ride away.
  "A lassie puir he will na' wed—
  Say never mair his name!" he said.

Sadly the filial lass obeyed—
But love would not be so gainsayed;
  Among her father's flowers, her tongue
  "Sweet William!" of its own self sung.

Her stern sire heard. She seized a flower
First blossomed in that very hour.
  "This do I mean!" she cried, ashamed.
  And so the bonny flower was named.

July 8, 1927

Riches

My purse today is empty,
  My bank-account is bare—
But my sweet-peas have blossomed
  And perfume all the air.

The trellis by my window
  With pastel hues is spread,
With lavender and purple,
  With cream and pink and red.

The honey-bees have found them,
  The butterflies alight,
The humming-birds surround them
  A-flutter with delight.

No riches could buy fairer
  Or sweeter flowers than these.
I have wealth today—I own
  A rainbow of sweet-peas!

JULY 19, 1927

Help Yourself!

Sweet are blackberries from the vine,
   Fresh with dew and sun.
Air and appetite combine
   To season every one.

Fruits have flavor on the bough,
   Lost to dish and table.
Climb your plum trees, children, now,
   While your limbs are able!

Currants eaten as they grow
   Taste like liquid honey.
Gooseberries, like emeralds glow
   From their hedges sunny.

And these the choicest nectar yield,
   So it seems to me:
Watermelons in the field—
   And cherries on the tree!

JULY 20, 1927

A Problem

My flowers are lovely out of doors,
In settings natural, of course;
   So lovely that I'm scarcely able
   To pick them to adorn my table!

I stand before the crimson phlox,
The delicate blue four-o'clocks,
   My scissors flashing in the sun,
   And just can't bear to snip a one!

But in the house, the rooms demand
Posies on each vacant stand.
   I picture roses here and there,
   And clematis hanging o'er the stair.

They fade and wilt so soon inside—
How rob my garden of its pride!
   Now how to manage! What to do!
   To pick my flowers—and have them too!

AUGUST 15, 1927

After the Rain

The world has had its dusty face
   Washed clean.
The rain removed all sooty trace
   And left fresh green.

Each shrub, each blade of grass, each flower
   Along the path,
Under the rain's sweet-scented shower
   Has had its bath.

Like some cloud-tangled, ribboned mop,
   The warm, wet breeze
Has shined my roof from eaves to top
   And scoured the trees.

Old Mother Nature's on the run
   In her brisk way.
She'll finish up with wind and sun
   Her scrubbing day!

AUGUST 16, 1927

The Secret Gardeners

They said my peach tree wouldn't bloom
  Because of early April frost.
"You set it out too soon," they said,
  "And now your work and time are lost."

Then May came in, with ground aflame
  With crocuses and daffodils,
With wind-flowers and with dogwood flung
  Like perfume on the singing hills.

My peach tree bloomed! A great bouquet,
  It stood rose-misted like a bride.
But I had known—for I had seen
  Three secret gardeners at its side.

One moonlit night I saw them there,
  Gardeners gentle as a dove,
Nursing my peach blooms into life.
  Their names were Faith and Hope and Love.

AUGUST 30, 1927

An Old-fashioned Bouquet

(Suggested by Mrs. L. B. E., Rochester, N.Y.)

There were yellow roses in it,
   There was heliotrope and phlox,
There were marigolds and asters
   And a spray of four o'clocks.

From her quaint old-fashioned garden
   Grandma took the bleeding-heart,
The pinks, the rose geranium
   With its odor spiced and tart.

There were dahlias and nasturtiums,
   And a single Marguerite,
With larkspur blue as June skies
   And lavender as sweet.

An old-fashioned bunch of posies,
   Picked and blended without art;
It faded twenty years ago—
   But still blooms in my heart!

OCTOBER 6, 1927

Night-Times

I love a blue night, full of silver stars;
  A warm night, murmurous with crickets' hum.
  I love the nights when wraithy Fall mists come;
The red moon rising o'er the pasture bars.

I love a clear-cut and a frosty night,
  With black pines pointed against white-iced snow.
  I love the night when shutters creak and blow,
Oak branches crash, and scurrying owls take flight.

But holy is the night with slow, soft rain,
  With wet roofs shining down the lamp-lit street;
  Peace in the passing splash of friendly feet—
My hearth-fire gleaming on my window-pane.

NOVEMBER 11, 1926

Winter Sun

There's not much of it—that may be
    Why it is welcome, since it's rare;
And why it seems a bar of gold,
    Lying across the table there.

Over my kitchen pots and pans
    It trails its shining finger-tips.
Spills over in the living-room,
    And in my hands, like honey, drips.

A Winter sun, like memory,
    Brings back the thought of Summer haze.
Remembrance of the birds and flowers,
    The ecstasy of August days.

A handful of such sun would seem
    All that the Heavens can afford,
In Winter-time. Consider me
    Most grateful for small favors, Lord!

JANUARY 5, 1927

INDEX OF POEMS